SOLI
DEO GLORIA

New Testament Studies
in Honor of William Childs Robinson

EDITED BY

J. McDOWELL RICHARDS

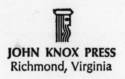

JOHN KNOX PRESS
Richmond, Virginia

Unless otherwise noted, and with the exception of occasional translations by the authors, Scripture quotations are from the *Revised Standard Version of the Bible,* copyrighted 1946 and 1952.

Library of Congress Catalog Card Number: 68-20620
© M. E. Bratcher 1968
Printed in the United States of America
23-0415

FOREWORD

It is not given to many men to teach in one institution for forty-one years. Smaller still is the number of those who have served for so long a period with such effectiveness and distinction as has the man in whose honor this volume is published—The Reverend William Childs Robinson, Professor of Church History, Church Polity and Apologetics at Columbia Theological Seminary. In recognition of this fact a group of Dr. Robinson's colleagues and former students decided months ago that no more appropriate tribute could be paid to their friend at the time of his retirement than the publication of a volume which would be a worthy contribution to the field of Christian scholarship. The essays contained in the pages which follow are testimony to the soundness of their planning and the effectiveness of their efforts.

The list of those who gladly responded to an invitation to contribute to the preparation of this volume is of such distinction as to need no lengthy comment here. Its outstanding merit and its international character will be noted at once by all who are familiar with theological scholarship in our times. England, Scotland, Germany, and Switzerland, as well as the United States of America, are represented by those who have helped to make possible the success of this undertaking.

The academic stature of these men commands respect for their writings, and Columbia Theological Seminary is both proud and grateful that they have united in honoring one of its most illustrious sons. It is high tribute to Dr. Robinson that he can claim such men as friends and that he holds their high respect as an associate and a fellow worker in the great task of theological education.

Worthy of particular comment is the fact that three of these writers are among his former students. Still more notable is the fact that two of these men—William C. Robinson, Jr., and James

M. Robinson—are products not only of his classroom but of his home. Each of these, his only sons, has now attained scholarly eminence and wide recognition in his own right. The fact that these men have followed their father into the ministry and into the field of theological teaching constitutes in itself a testimonial more significant than any which others could pay.

William Childs Robinson was born in Lincolnton, North Carolina, but from early childhood lived near the former campus of Columbia Theological Seminary in Columbia, South Carolina. Many of his early associations were with that "school of the prophets," its professors and its students. His father, David W. Robinson, was for years a devoted and useful member of the Board of Directors of the Seminary. A brother, David W. Robinson, Jr., and a sister, Mrs. R. C. (Alice Robinson) Johnson, also served the institution ably and unselfishly in legal and business relationships during the difficult days of what we know as the Great Depression.

After graduation from Roanoke College in Virginia, the young William entered Columbia Theological Seminary as a student and received his B.D. in 1920, while also fulfilling requirements for an M.A. from the University of South Carolina. He then entered Princeton Theological Seminary for a year of postgraduate study leading to his Th.M. He was later to earn his Th.D. at Harvard University and to receive an honorary Doctorate in Divinity from his collegiate Alma Mater.

In 1921 Dr. Robinson was married to Miss Mary McConkey of Salem, Virginia. In the same year he became pastor of the Presbyterian Church in Gettysburg, Pennsylvania, where he served effectively for five years. In him intellectual ability and scholarly instincts were combined with a deep pastoral concern. This fact is attested by the deep affection in which he has been held not only in Gettysburg but in at least eight other churches which he has served as a ministerial supply during his busy years as a teacher.

The first year of Dr. Robinson's tenure as professor in Columbia Theological Seminary was spent largely on leave of absence for study at Harvard University. Hence, his entrance upon full-time service as a teacher coincided with the institution's establishment upon what was then its new campus in Decatur, Georgia, in the fall of 1927. The early years in this location were not easy. The faculty and student body were small. After the stock market crash of 1929, it was by no means certain that the school would survive the financial difficulties which it faced. Faculty salaries, which were already inadequate, had to be drastically reduced. Serving—as did other professors at that time—upon a truly sacrificial basis, Dr. Robinson remained steadfast in the conviction that the institution had a mission to serve the Southeast and that it should decline offers to merge with seminaries elsewhere. The wisdom of that conviction has been attested by the events that have followed.

Columbia Theological Seminary's student body has grown from approximately sixty in number to more than two hundred since 1927. Its faculty has increased in size from six to twenty-two professors, and its library has grown in proportion. Through its sons the Seminary has already played a role of tremendous importance in the rapid growth of the church in the five southeastern states and beyond. The challenge and promise of its future are great. As a member of its faculty during all this period, Dr. Robinson has made an important contribution to the growth and welfare of the institution.

Of the more than twenty-three hundred graduates of this school, approximately fourteen hundred are now living. The most of these have graduated since 1927 and hence have received a significant part of their training from Dr. Robinson. Through them, his influence extends today not only throughout the United States but to many other lands.

As a teacher and as a churchman, Dr. Robinson has not sought for popularity. A diligent scholar himself, he has expected hard work of his students, in some of whom at least he has inspired a new concept of and devotion to scholarship. A man of deep conviction concerning the centralities of the Christian faith, he has steadfastly sought to oppose error as he saw it, and to bear witness to truth as revealed in Scripture and in Jesus Christ. Such teaching has not always been received with enthusiasm by his hearers. But while some of these may disagree with Dr. Robinson on details, there are few indeed who have not come to respect him deeply as a scholar, a teacher, and a Christian. Many a man who sat in his classes has a more vertebrate theology, a higher regard for the church, and a deeper sense of mission because of the instruction received.

Among the books written by Dr. Robinson are *Columbia Theological Seminary and The Southern Presbyterian Church; The Certainties of the Gospel; What Is Christian Faith?; The Word of the Cross; Our Lord, an Affirmation of the Deity of Christ; Christ the Hope of Glory; Christ the Bread of Life;* and *The Reformation—A Rediscovery of Grace.* He has also had a part in the preparation of other significant books and translations and has been a constant contributor to various theological journals and church publications. His ability has been recognized by invitations to deliver the Free Church Lectures in Edinburgh, the Sprunt Lectures at Union Theological Seminary in Virginia, the Payton Lectures at Fuller Theological Seminary, the R. L. Robinson Lectures at Erskine Theological Seminary, and the Alumni Lectures at Columbia Theological Seminary. He has also taught several courses at the Candler School of Theology of Emory University.

The titles of this man's writings indicate the emphases of his thought and his teaching. As an exponent and a champion of the Reformed faith he has sought to sound again and again the vital affirmations of the Protestant Reformation. In doing this he has emphasized always the authority of the Word of God and the Lordship of Jesus Christ. For him the fact of the sovereignty of God has been central, and he has constantly taught and preached the doctrine of justification by faith—"By grace are ye saved through faith; and that not of yourselves: it is the gift of God."

It is not likely that Dr. Robinson, or any other reader, will agree with all that is contained in this book. Of one thing, however, we may be sure. He will approve of its title, for this represents the witness of his life—the goal of his endeavor as a minister, a scholar, a writer, and a teacher.

Soli Deo Gloria—To God alone be the glory.

J. McDowell Richards
Decatur, Georgia

CONTENTS

I

THE RELEVANCE OF REDEMPTIVE HISTORY

Oscar Cullmann

TRANSLATED BY JOHN A. HARE

Today, when the predominant tendency among Protestant and Catholic theologians is to bring forward *aggiornamento,** is it justifiable to speak of *redemptive history*? Does speaking of redemptive history not bring forward an outmoded concept? Is this not falling back into the conservatism existing prior to the Council? I shall endeavor to show here that such is not the case. There is a false *aggiornamento* which abandons the substance of the gospel. The true *aggiornamento* is that which, on the contrary, renders comprehensible to the modern world not what the world already knows, but precisely the substance of the gospel.

The theological innovation of the Council was to return to the dynamism of redemptive history as the Bible makes it known to us, and to discover the *dynamic* continuity between the action of God in the past and his action in the present and future. The great theological renewal of the Council consists in this, that the static concepts of scholasticism are abandoned in order to place in the foreground a dynamic theology which is that of redemptive history properly understood.

This is the way the great theologians of the recent Council understood their task, and we see the results in the various decrees and constitutions. Pope Paul VI also, in replying to the statement of the non-Catholic observers in an audience granted them at the beginning of the second session, said that he willingly subscribed

---

* Translator's Note: *aggiornamento,* literally, "updating"; specifically, the effort and desire to make relevant to the modern world the substance of the gospel by expressing it in modern terminology and forms.

"to a concrete and historic theology centered upon redemptive history," and that he would encourage studies pursuing this goal in one of the existing institutions or if necessary establish a new institute for this purpose.[†]

Redemptive history thus is not only the element of renewal in Catholic theology, but is also the basis of the ecumenical dialogue. But we should first of all ask: What is redemptive history?

WHAT IS REDEMPTIVE HISTORY?

The role which history plays in Christianity becomes immediately evident. In Christianity redemption depends upon a divine act which the Christian considers as the central divine act. This is Jesus Christ, dead and resurrected. And this act has been accomplished within the framework of history. This essential fact perhaps distinguishes Christianity from other religions. Only in Judaism is the historical element equally of fundamental importance; however, Jewish redemptive history is not concentrated upon *one single* central event as is the case with Christian redemptive history. The latter, moreover, adapts the history of Israel but orients it entirely toward this center—the historical fact of Jesus Christ, his incarnation, his life upon earth, his crucifixion, and his resurrection. To be sure, it is not sufficient to envisage the historical part of this event only within the framework of secular history. Its importance for the Christian faith transcends by far the framework of secular history. It is not only the center of all history, it is also the center of all divine action through which God makes himself known to the world and reveals himself to us. He reveals himself to us not only within the history of men, but also within the history of creation. The history of creation and the history of mankind form a part of what we call redemptive history. On this point I agree with Teilhard de Chardin: redemptive history has a cosmic scope (the work of Jesus Christ). But the center of all this redemptive history is the incarnation of Jesus Christ within the framework of human history. The effect of this fact transcends the history of humanity, but it *inserts itself* into this history.

[†] This institute has just been created in Jerusalem.

The center of the Christian faith is not of a metaphysical order, but rather of a historical order. That is why the conciliar constitution *De Divina Revelatione* rightly emphasizes the fact that it is not necessary to *deny* the historical character of the facts spoken of by the Gospels.

The center of the Christian faith is an event of history. But in saying *center* we are presupposing that the plane on which God reveals himself to us has a horizontal extension in time. The supreme revelation is the event of Jesus Christ. In him are concentrated at the same time the fullness of the complete development of redemption and the complete *meaning* of this development. But that which is signified by the central event of Christ, that which is concentrated in this event, is displayed. It is displayed *before* the event in making ready for it, and it is displayed *after* the event in explaining it. There is therefore a *plan* of God, a plan of redemption, which is unfolded in time according to his divine will. In my book *Christ and Time,* written more than twenty years ago, I stressed the fact that time, of which God is the master and of which the Bible speaks, is not an element resulting from the Fall, but rather is a means of grace which God uses to make himself known to the world and to offer us redemption. I insisted upon "linear" time which the biblical redemptive history presupposes, as opposed to the cyclical time of the Greeks in which everything returns to its beginning and in which deliverance consequently consists in being delivered out of time. No such idea as the latter appears in Christianity, in which redemption is accomplished by God within time.

In my new book, *Le Salut dans l'Histoire,* I maintain this conception; however, I correct it on one important point. I had formerly spoken of a *straight* line and a rectilinear development. Today I continue to say *line,* but I state *curved line.* For in redemptive history there are movements—resulting from the human revolt against the plan of God, resulting from sin—which move in the opposite direction; but God is able to cause good to result from evil. This is what the Apostle Paul expresses in Romans 3, where he says that our infidelity cannot nullify the fidelity of God. And again in Romans 9-11 he shows that the skepticism of the Jews served to cause the pagans to enter into the Christian Church; yet just the same, the plan of God with regard to Israel is not abandoned. In the end Israel will be converted. Therefore God pursues his plan of redemption in spite of human opposition. What I thus develop in my book Paul Claudel has marvelously expressed by a Portuguese proverb which he has had inscribed in his *Soulier de satin*: "God writes straight, but in *curved* lines."

In this brief outline of what we mean by redemptive history two aspects of this history must still be considered. It is not necessary to believe that all of secular history is redemptive history in the strict sense of the word. For instance, not all the history of ancient man forms redemptive history. According to the faith of the men of the Bible, God has chosen certain events even as he has chosen, "elected," certain men—and a people, Israel, in order that she fulfill a particular mission for all mankind. Thus biblical history is not a history which proceeds chronologically without interruption. There are chronological lacunae by virtue of the choice of which I have just spoken. God chooses certain events. There is even a progressive reduction which moves from the whole of creation to mankind charged with a mission for creation, and from mankind to Israel. Since Israel as a whole does not fulfill her mission, the reduction continues. God chooses a remnant—the remnant of which the prophets speak—and the reduction is continued on down to the One, Jesus Christ, who substitutes himself for all mankind. Beginning with him there is an inverse movement from the One to the band of disciples, from the band of disciples to the church, from the church to mankind. Thus the objective of redemptive history is the whole of mankind. The means chosen by God to attain this is that of the election of a minority, of substitution. Therefore we can say that there is in the strict sense a redemptive history which represents only the narrow line of which the Bible speaks, and there is in the larger sense a redemptive history which includes the history of mankind and also that of the whole of creation.

The second point to be raised is closely connected with the first. There are at the same time in redemptive history a horizontal action and a vertical action of God. The vertical action is integrated into the divine plan of horizontal action. I emphasize this point because of the criticisms directed to me charging that everything is considered exclusively from the aspect of horizontal action. This charge is not correct. I emphasize that the central event, Jesus Christ, is truly itself a vertical event, but one which thrusts itself into a horizontal plane.

Such therefore, outlined in a concise manner, is my conception of redemptive history as I believe it to be found in the Bible. I stress this last phrase, "in the Bible," because there was in the history of Protestant theology in the last century a German school called "the school of redemptive history." It was entirely dominated by the philosophy of Hegel. In contrast to this school I have endeavored to present redemptive history as strictly and closely connected with the exegesis of the Bible and always from this perspective.

Certain of my students would wish to make me a theological leader—a *chef d'école*. I refuse this. Redemptive history is for me a thing far too important to become the descriptive phrase and slogan of a theological school. Redemptive history is the heart of all theology which is based upon the Bible. It represents an essential aspect of all theology. It is the perspective from which the very objects of all Christian theology, God and Christ, are seen. Obviously the objects of theology are God and Christ, but the perspective from which they are viewed is not that of metaphysical or existentialist speculation, but rather that of redemptive history.

The very fact that the basis of revelation is the Bible proves that it is not a question of a "school," but rather is nothing more than a question of Christianity. How are we to justify the biblical canon—that is, the union of the New Testament with the Old Testament—as the norm otherwise than by the history of redemption? Why is the New Testament preceded by the Old Testament in our Bible? In addition, when we consider our church today—her worship, her liturgy—is she not wholly inspired by *redemptive history*? We see this in our church calendar: Advent, Christmas, Palm Sunday, Passion Week, Good Friday, Easter, Pentecost.

THE ROLE OF REDEMPTIVE HISTORY
IN THE THEOLOGY OF THE PAST CENTURIES

After having seen what redemptive history is according to the Bible, let us now quickly examine the attempts which have been made over the centuries to eliminate precisely what forms the very *heart* of all redemptive history, namely, the historical element. This elimination reduces redemptive history to a metaphysical truth according to ancient philosophy, or to an existential experience according to modern philosophy. In antiquity the attempt was undertaken by Gnosticism. All historians agree in admitting that if Gnosticism had triumphed in early Christianity, it would have been the end of Christianity. Indeed, then the fate of Christianity would have been the same as that of all other religions. It would have collapsed as they did in a vast syncretism. Philosophical syncretism, in order to absorb all religions into its philosophical system, had to strip them of all historical elements. Two religions proved intractable to this attempt. These two—Judaism and Christianity—by their very *essence* are based upon a redemptive history. That is why they are the only ones which have survived. The Gnostic attack against redemptive history was therefore an attack against the existence of *Christianity* itself. This is what was understood by the church fathers who fought heresy and who, above all St. Irenaeus, combated the Gnostics. They fought for a theology of redemptive history in order to save the Christian faith. Such is indeed the meaning of that battle. The great theologians of antiquity recognized that the heresy *par excellence* is the elimination of redemptive history. That is why the foremost heresy, combated previously in the New Testament, is Docetism, for it wishes to eliminate the historical element from the doctrine relating to Christ.

Yes, such was the meaning of that great battle in early Christianity, and we must also be vigilant today with regard to the present theological tendencies which we see being poured out into both Protestant theology and Catholic theology. On the pretext that it is necessary to render the gospel comprehensible to the modern world, the attempt is made, time and time again, to eliminate redemptive history by considering it simply as a secondary expression, not in the least essential, of a truth concerning our existence. Time and time again they sacrifice redemptive history to a philosophy, to the "modern world," which becomes the modern idol. I want to speak of the German school which attaches itself to the name of the great German theologian, Bultmann. I say "great theologian," for I accept all that he has done with the philological and historical point of view on the exegetical plane, but I consider as theologically disastrous his program of demythologization. If it were truly only a question of demythologization—that is, the elimination of true myths—I would accept it willingly, for we are aware that there *are* mythical elements in the Bible. But it is a question of something else with Bultmann: the dehistorization of the Bible for the benefit of the philosophy of Heidegger. For Bultmann and his disciples, who venture still further than he, redemptive history would be a distortion of the message of the gospel, which they regard as in reality a Christian existentialism. Luke is said to have invented redemptive history, and in doing this to have distorted the gospel in the direction of Catholicism. (Käsemann formerly even proposed to eliminate Luke from the canon and has spoken of the common error of Luke and Cullmann.) Redemptive history would then be an "objectification" of the evangelical message which would in reality concern only an experience of faith, an experience relating to the understanding of our existence. Theology is therefore reduced to anthropology. I see therein a danger fully as great as that of Gnosticism in antiquity—the absorption of the gospel by a philosophy. Only today it is no longer a question of Greek philosophy, but of existentialist philosophy.

I confess my astonishment that Catholic theologians in Europe and especially in the United States have let themselves be influenced in their turn by that theological school. There is a kind of flirtation by some Catholic theologians with Bultmann's theology. I do not have to instruct Catholic theology. But since it is, at the outset, a matter of a Protestant theory which they submit to their influence, I feel authorized in addressing to them this warning: Do not accept that which is most problematical. It is especially necessary to beware of an ecumenicity based upon the abandonment of the substance of the gospel for the benefit of the modern world. To be sure, it is necessary to preach the gospel to the modern world—but truly the gospel. It is not necessary to preach to the world what the world says to itself and what it says even better than we. I am convinced that too many theologians on both sides are in reality "*ashamed* of the gospel," to use the words of Paul. They capitulate to the world. They think that redemptive history is a thing which is now outmoded and which concerns solely the past. They forget that our norm must be the gospel and not the modern world. "Do not be conformed to this world," says the apostle (Romans 12).

THE LESSON FOR OUR DAY

There is a false *aggiornamento* by which we compromise the true *aggiornamento* which, to be sure, must remain our great task and our constant preoccupation. The progressives themselves are the ones who must react against the false *aggiornamento*. They must not leave this reaction against radicalism to the *status quo ante* conservatives alone, for their reaction is obviously bad.

Redemptive history properly understood is not solely an *outmoded history* of interest only to archaeologists and historians. To the contrary, I would like to show that it is an eminently relevant and present matter. A theology based on redemptive history is more relevant than a theology based on a philosophical conceptuality. In the past was it not precisely a much too radical adaptation to the world which often, in Catholicism, estranged theological thought from its vital source, the Bible, and which thus removed from theology theology's "actual" nature? For biblical redemptive history has this great quality of always remaining relevant and never becoming outmoded.

If God realizes redemption for us within history, it follows that our *present* time, included in the period between the terrestrial advent of Christ and his parousia at the end of the age, forms a part of this very same history. In this lies the reason for the dynamic character of the faith and consequently of the theological thought also of the first Christians. They had the conviction of being—along with their time, however hostile it was to the gospel—within this great stream of a divine history, a divine plan which has been realized before us and which will be accomplished in the end. Our time shares in this. To be sure, we do not have a charter which tells us what is strictly redemptive history in the present time. Not everything is redemptive history in the events which we see unfolding around us. The *norm* of redemptive history for today is given us only indirectly in the Bible, which speaks to us on the one hand of the biblical history of Israel, of the life of Jesus, and of the birth of the church; and on the other hand, of the events of the last days. But this norm does not expressly describe the events of the intermediate time—this present time in which we live and which is the time of the church. And yet it is remarkable that the Bible contains the book of Acts (which certain students of Bultmann would like to eliminate from the Bible). The book of Acts speaks to us precisely about the beginning of the first phase of this intermediate time in which we now live.

We therefore have a norm by which to judge, most certainly with prudence, our time and to discover in it the unfolding of the divine plan—"the divine economy." It should not be said that this norm no longer can be applied to our time, an age dominated by technology. Most certainly our time is totally different from that into which the gospel entered. It is, however, quite necessary to realize that the secular world then also had difficulty in understanding the gospel. It was hardly any easier for the modern man of that day—for example, the philosophers of Athens—to understand it than it is for the modern man of today. On the Areopagus the Athenians laughed when Paul spoke of the resurrection of a man, Jesus Christ. But Paul did not, as a consequence of that laughter, draw the conclusion that he should from then on declare that the resurrection was a myth to be eliminated. If he had preached a demythologized gospel such as certain theologians present nowadays, the Athenians indeed would not have laughed; but it would no longer have been the gospel.

Our situation *with regard to the gospel* is not therefore so radically different from that of the world in the beginning of our era as it is said to be, and the Bible can remain our norm in order that we also may discover in our time the action of God by placing the newspaper next to the Bible and the Bible next to the newspaper.

Our time is in this great living and dynamic stream which is redemptive history. That is the *true* relevance of theology. It is not relevance based on the abandonment of fundamental principles. The pagan world and the non-Christian religions are entirely within the perspective of this history, and redemptive history is relevant in this regard also. I mention again that the *means* employed by God to realize redemptive history is reduction —the election of a minority for the redemption of all. The objective, however, is the world of the pagans. It is the universe. In the end all peoples and all things will be integrated into this history.

THE ECUMENICAL NATURE OF
REDEMPTIVE HISTORY

I stated at the outset that a theology of redemptive history is particularly appropriate to serve as the basis for ecumenical dialogue between Protestants and Catholics. But why? Precisely because of its truly relevant nature; because the present time is *integrated* into the great stream of redemptive history. It is no accident that as soon as the texts were expressed in the categories of redemptive history we could be certain of speaking a common language with the Council. We Protestants and Catholics may appear to be separated precisely on the question of knowing whether or not redemptive history continues in the present time. Formerly we often said that for Protestants redemptive history terminated with the Bible, whereas for the Catholics it continues in the church. That was an error which stemmed from the fact that on the Protestant side the idea of redemptive history was not examined thoroughly enough. The *revelation* concerning redemptive history indeed draws to a close with the time of the apostles; but redemptive history itself does not. Here, then, is a tenet the importance of which for the ecumenical dialogue cannot be overestimated. The basis for our ecumenical conversation widens considerably as soon as both sides admit that our present time, the time of the church, is an integral part of redemptive history.

To be sure, the problems which still divide us are not resolved that way. But we have then a common basis for discussion. The problems are not resolved, because we remain radically separated on the question which characterizes this intermediate time—namely, that of the infallibility of the church and of tradition. On the Protestant side we maintain that the intermediate time with its tradition cannot have the same normative value as the Bible in that which relates to revelation, and we emphasize the possibility of the church's error on not only the moral plane but also the doctrinal plane. But in spite of the differences, we will approach all these problems in a framework more favorable to discussion if we place ourselves resolutely upon this common foundation which is the integration of the present age of the church into a history which began before us and will continue after us unto the end.

But it remains for us to reply to a few objections arising for the most part from what I call the false *aggiornamento*. The first objection asks: In what way can this redemptive history concern me personally? It has been said that only the theology of Bultmann based upon the existentialism of Heidegger and emphasizing the necessity for personal decision would be appropriate today to give each of us the moral élan needed in his life. The theology of redemptive history, on the other hand, would not imply an ethic. To this difficulty it is necessary to answer that, to the contrary, the theology of redemptive history calls us to integrate ourselves, to integrate our personal lives, *in this history*. It calls us to recognize in each moment the personal duty which is assigned us at the exact spot and in the exact instant where God has placed each of us. Most certainly it is necessary that we make a decision, as Bultmann says; but, like the early Christians, we resolve to *integrate* ourselves along with all our personal problems into the divine plan which has been revealed to us.

All of us in the modest place where each is found must be aware of being the divine instruments of this plan. The conviction of being the instruments of a divine plan ought to confer upon all our actions, whatever be their success or momentary failure, the same joy and assurance which inspired the early Christians.

A second objection asks: Is it true that the Bible is essentially a series of events, a history of redemption? Does it not first of all contain teachings, the divine *word*? It is true that there is in the Bible, next to the events, the divine *word*. But this divine word is inseparable from the divine event. It is absolutely contrary to biblical thought to oppose the word of God and the act of God. In speaking, God acts; and conversely, in each of his acts, God makes himself known and reveals himself to the world. He "speaks." Each divine act is a divine word. "Let there be light, and there was light." Thus in Hebrew, the word which signifies "utterance" is the expression for history—*debarim*. In addition, the supreme revelation of God, Jesus incarnate and all the works which he accomplished, is called *logos*—"word." The Holy Spirit acts by speaking, and he speaks by acting. There are no grounds for opposing the word of God and redemptive history. And this brings us to a last question which is debated to such a degree in our present discussions following from the program of demythologization for which Bultmann has given the watchword. I have already said that for Bultmann redemptive history would be, in the final analysis, only the mythical expression of an encounter between the man of today and God. Everything would be only myth, and the question therefore would be one of demythologizing the Bible in order to release from it the existentialist nucleus—our understanding of ourselves. We reply by saying it is true that the Bible contains mythical elements, in particular in Genesis and also in certain parts of other books. But the role of these mythical elements is not the one attributed to them by the school of Bultmann—namely, the description of our personal existence. The Bible, by placing myth and history upon the same plane, imposes on us the task of distinguishing one from the other, and not to say with the school of Bultmann that everything is only myth. No, it is necessary to distinguish between them, and *it is necessary to recognize* that there are mythical elements. Even then the theology of redemptive history by no means escapes from the actual problems. For the Bible, by placing myths side by side with history, has *not* wanted to subordinate, so to speak, all history to myth as is the case with Bultmann; but to the contrary it has subordinated myth to history. The role of the myth is to explain to us the *meaning of redemptive history,* to make conspicuous precisely the reason why God has caused to unfold for us and our redemption this history wholly concentrated in Jesus Christ who is its summit and point of orientation—Jesus Christ, dead and resurrected for us.

Finally I shall mention an objection addressed to me which would be serious if it were accurate. It has been said that I would replace faith in the Trinity with faith in redemptive history. This is entirely to misapprehend my thought. I have already said, and I emphasize it on each page of my book, that Jesus Christ is the center of our faith, and that in him all divine action is concentrated. But it has pleased God to unfold, *in revealing himself* to us, his highest revelation and act of supreme grace which he gives us in Jesus Christ. We understand much better who God is, who Christ is, who the Holy Spirit is— in short, that which is the Trinity—precisely when we do not enclose our theology within the framework of static concepts, but when we view it from the perspective of the Bible, namely, the dynamism of revelation within redemptive history. The Trinity is revealed to us according to the divine will—it is expressed in redemptive history.

In every way redemptive history, far from interesting only the past and driving us back to an outmoded position, is an element of life which urges us forward, because it is capable of placing our modern time with all its prodigious progress within the continuity of a past history and the perspective of a future history. It places us individually over and above the ages, within the succession of the humble Christians of the first century who, in their humility and in spite of their small numbers, nevertheless had the joyous assurance of having fulfilled a great task for the world. It is precisely after having surveyed redemptive history in Romans 9-11 that the Apostle Paul exults with joy and his thought is transformed into prayer: "O the depth of the riches and wisdom and knowledge of God!" It was this joy which sustained him in his missionary work. It can be ours.

II

"JESUS IS LORD"

F. F. Bruce

I

For Paul, a Christian is a man who acknowledges that "Jesus is Lord" ($\kappa\acute{\upsilon}\rho\iota\sigma\varsigma$ '$I\eta\sigma\sigma\hat{\upsilon}\varsigma$), with corresponding faith in his heart. No one can utter such words except by the power of the Holy Spirit (1 Cor. 12:3); to everyone who utters them, believing in his heart that God raised Jesus from the dead, salvation is assured (Rom. 10:9). The parallelism between outward confession and inward faith in the latter passage implies that "Jesus is Lord" and "God has raised him from the dead" are two ways of saying the same thing. It is as the risen one that Jesus is Lord.

The contexts in which the confession "Jesus is Lord" appears imply that Paul is not coining this formula—they imply, indeed, that whoever may have coined it, it was not Paul. The implication is that he is quoting a common Christian form of *homologia*.

It has been argued (e.g., by W. Kramer[1]) that, since the expanded form of the confession found in Philippians 2:11, "Jesus Christ is Lord" ($\kappa\acute{\upsilon}\rho\iota\sigma\varsigma$ '$I\eta\sigma\sigma\hat{\upsilon}\varsigma$ $\chi\rho\iota\sigma\tau\acute{\sigma}\varsigma$), suggests a Hellenistic origin— since it was in the Hellenistic and not in the Semitic-speaking world that $\chi\rho\iota\sigma\tau\acute{\sigma}\varsigma$ came to be used as practically the name, or part of the name, of Jesus—a Hellenistic origin must be ascribed to $\kappa\acute{\upsilon}\rho\iota\sigma\varsigma$ '$I\eta\sigma\sigma\hat{\upsilon}\varsigma$. This does not follow. Where a Greek-speaking Christian said $\kappa\acute{\upsilon}\rho\iota\sigma\varsigma$ '$I\eta\sigma\sigma\hat{\upsilon}\varsigma$, an Aramaic-speaking Christian could equally well say *mar Yēšūaʿ*—or, if he wished to be more emphatic, *Yēšūaʿ hū'mārē* (or *māryā*). Every shade of meaning which a Greek-speaking Christian gave to $\kappa\acute{\upsilon}\rho\iota\sigma\varsigma$ could be given by an Aramaic-speaking Christian to *mar*. In any case, too much is sometimes made of the distinction between Hellenistic and Palestinian (or "Hebrew") Christianity in the apostolic age. In the first century A.D., Palestine had been part of the Hellenistic world for three or four centuries, and even those of its inhabitants who spoke Aramaic were influenced by Hellenistic culture, just as (conversely) one who spoke and wrote Greek could, like Paul, call himself "a Hebrew born of Hebrews" (Phil. 3:5; cf. 2 Cor. 11:22).

For all his insistence on the confession κύριος Ἰησοῦς, however, Paul was no formalist; he would not demand the use of one invariable formula. Any other expression that served the same purpose would be acceptable, and κύριος had a variety of synonyms. Thus, in Romans 1:4, where perhaps also a pre-Pauline confession is echoed, Jesus in resurrection is appointed *Son of God* "in power." Again (to go beyond the Pauline writings), if for Paul the confession "Jesus is Lord" assures salvation, for John the belief that "Jesus is the Christ" is a token that one is a child of God (1 John 5:1), and the Fourth Gospel is written in order that its readers "may believe that Jesus is the Christ, the Son of God"—and believing have life in his name (John 20:31). Lord, Christ, Son of God—these are near synonyms: to believe that Jesus is one of these is to believe that he is all of these, and all of them are given to him as the risen and exalted one.

To other New Testament writers also Jesus is Lord. He is so in James (1:1; 2:1), in 1 Peter (1:3; 3:15), 2 Peter (1:2, 8, etc.), and Jude (4, 17, 21, 25); to the writer to the Hebrews he is "our Lord" (7:14) and to the seer of Patmos he is "Lord of lords" (17:14; 19:16).

Another body of evidence is constituted by the early speeches in Acts. In them no great theological weight is laid on the death of Jesus, even when (as in 3:13 ff.) he is presented as the Servant. The emphasis is on his resurrection and exaltation as the divine act of vindication which reversed the humiliation and suffering inflicted on him by his human judges who disallowed his claims. It is in this vindication that God gives notice that the crucified Jesus is now both Lord and Messiah (2:36), as well as the glorified Servant (3:13), the prophet like Moses (3:22-23), the headstone of the corner (4:11), a Leader and Savior to give Israel repentance and remission of sins (5:31; cf. 10:43), and the coming Judge of the living and the dead (10:42).

This presentation is corroborated by the opening clauses of

Romans where Paul (as has been said) seems to quote an established
form of confessional language which speaks of one who was born
of David's line according to the flesh but appointed Son of God
in power according to the spirit—according to the *Holy* Spirit—
by the resurrection from the dead: namely, Jesus Christ our Lord
(Rom. 1:3-4); it is corroborated further by a quasi-hymnic passage
later in the letter which refers to "Christ Jesus, who died . . . [rather]
who was raised from the dead, who is at the right hand of God, who
indeed intercedes for us" (Rom. 8:34). Although this last quotation
does not include the term κύριος, it does present the substance of
that term as used of Jesus, for it is as the exalted one that Jesus
is κύριος.

More emphatic still to this effect is the probably pre-Pauline
hymn of Philippians 2:6 ff. where, after the description of the
humiliation of Jesus to the point of death by crucifixion, his vindication is celebrated thus: "Therefore God has highly exalted him
[cf. Acts 3:13] and bestowed on him the name which is above every
name, that at the name of Jesus every knee should bow, in heaven
and on earth and under the earth, and every tongue confess that
Jesus Christ is κύριος." Reference has already been made to the
form of this confession, and we shall return to consider further
implications of the hymn; for the moment, it suffices to note that
the bestowal on Jesus of the supreme title κύριος is the climax of his
exaltation.

II

We turn now to various strands of the gospel tradition.

In addition to κύριος, a number of other designations of lordship
are applied to Jesus in the Gospels, ἐπιστάτης, διδάσκαλος, and the
untranslated *rabbi* and *rabbuni*. The last two are Hebrew or Aramaic
titles of respect, given especially to a religious teacher, and διδάσκαλος
certainly and ἐπιστάτης probably are used as their Greek equiva-
lents. Occasionally they are used in the third person—for example,
in the message or password to be given to the owner of the *cenaculum*
in Mark 14:14 ("The Teacher says . . . ") or in Martha's words to
Mary in John 11:28 ("The Teacher is here . . ."). This is just the
way in which the friends of Jesus would have talked about him

during his ministry; behind the Greek wording we may safely recognize the Semitic "The rabbi." In Mark 11:3, however, where Jesus gives his disciples another password to be used when they are challenged for untying the colt on which he is to ride into Jerusalem, the term used thus in the third person is κύριος: "If any one says to you, 'Why are you doing this?' say, 'The Lord has need of it and will send it back here immediately.' " Perhaps the implication is that Jesus is the colt's real κύριος, in the sense in which Isaiah 1:3 LXX calls the ass's owner its κύριος; more probably ὁ κύριος in Mark 11:3 and parallels is simply a variant Greek rendering of "the rabbi."

For the most part, however, διδάσκαλος in the Gospels is applied to Jesus in the vocative, and ἐπιστάτης is always so applied (and exclusively in the Gospel of Luke). The vocatives διδάσκαλε and ἐπιστάτα are not only interchangeable the one with the other; as addressed to Jesus they are also interchangeable with the vocative κύριε. Thus, when the panic-stricken disciples rouse Jesus from sleep during the storm on the lake, they call him διδάσκαλε in Mark 4:38, ἐπιστάτα ἐπιστάτα in Luke 8:24, and κύριε in Matthew 8:25. The vocative κύριε was, and is, a common courtesy title in Greek, and no theological significance can be attached to its application to Jesus in the Gospels and Acts, whether we regard *rabbi* or *mārī* as its Aramaic substratum.

Apart from the use of κύριος referring to Jesus in the third person in Mark 11:3, we have Jesus' statement in Mark 2:28 and parallels that "the Son of man is κύριος even of the sabbath." In resurrection, Jesus is referred to as "the κύριος" by angels in Matthew 28:6 and by disciples in Luke 24:34. In Luke's nativity narrative Elizabeth calls Mary "the mother of my κύριος" before the birth of Jesus (Luke 1:43) and the herald angels proclaim the birth of "a Savior, who is χριστὸς κύριος"[2] (Luke 2:11). But when it comes to the Evangelists' personal description of Jesus as "the κύριος" in the course of their narratives, Luke emerges as the one most given to this usage. Fourteen times he speaks of Jesus as "the Lord" and once, in his resurrection narrative, as "the Lord Jesus" (Luke 24:3). This usage forms a contrast with the rarity of such usage on the part of Jesus' contemporaries; Luke calls him the Lord because for him the one of whom he writes these things is now the exalted one. This usage is much commoner in Luke than in John. In the first part of the Gospel of John, Jesus is called "the κύριος" three times, all in sentences which on quite independent grounds have been regarded as editorial notes (4:1; 6:23; 11:2). In John 13:13-14 Jesus himself tells his disciples in an *ad hominem* argument that if they call him their διδάσκαλος and κύριος, as they rightly do (the nominative, not the vocative, of *oratio recta* is used), they should follow his example of service. Otherwise the designation occurs in John's resurrection narrative. It is used by the Evangelist twice (20:20; 21:12), by Mary Magdalene three times (20:2, 13, 18; in verse 13 she calls Jesus "my Lord"), by the beloved disciple to Peter (21:7), by the other disciples to Thomas (20:25), and, as a climax, by Thomas himself in his confession "My Lord and my God!" (20:28), where again the nominative is used. Here Thomas is not addressing Jesus but is acknowledging his identity as the risen and exalted one.

The evidence of all the New Testament strata leads to the conclusion that the title κύριος belongs to Jesus as the one whom God has raised from the dead and enthroned alongside himself.

III

It has recently been maintained that although the title κύριος, in the existing New Testament writings, is overwhelmingly associated with the exaltation of Jesus, it was originally associated with his imminent parousia.[3] One plank in this argument is provided by Acts 3:19-21, a passage which has been thought to present "the most primitive Christology of all," to quote J. A. T. Robinson (although he adds a question mark after these words).[4] There the promise is given that, if the people of Jerusalem repent of their misguided rejection of Jesus, God will bring them the predicted "times of refreshing" and send them Jesus, their appointed (προκεχειρισμένος) Messiah, "whom heaven must receive until the time for establishing all that God spoke by the mouth of his holy prophets from of old" (cf. Luke 1:70).

Here, it is said, all the emphasis is on the parousia as the time when Jesus will be invested with Messiahship. But the participle προκεχειρισμένος does not demand this interpretation; it may as easily convey the same idea as is expressed in Acts 2:36—namely, that Jesus has been installed as messianic king by his being received into heaven (from which, it is declared in Acts 3:20, his people may expect his reappearance). Acts 3:19–21 may indeed be extremely primitive—possibly an application to Jesus of an earlier form of expectant phraseology directed toward Elijah.[5] But if, at this primitive stage, the vindication of Jesus denoted by his going to God on the clouds of heaven was regarded as fulfilled in his ascension,[6] then his now being in the presence of God, rather than his future return in itself, was the most important fact, and that which proclaimed his lordship. The parousia would but consummate the reign already fully inaugurated.

It is true that in the speech of Acts 3:13–26 Jesus is presented as Servant of the Lord, Prophet and Messiah, and not explicitly as κύριος. But κύριος and Messiah imply each other.

If we try to find evidence for the shift from the alleged earlier association of κύριος with the parousia to its association with Jesus' exaltation, we shall have to date it very early indeed. The Lordship of Jesus is associated with his exaltation and session at God's right hand in the earliest accessible confessional formulae; Romans 8:34 and 1 Peter 3:22 will serve as examples. (Whatever the date of these letters may be, the confessional language which they quote is much earlier and was common Christian property.) If Psalm 110:1 played the part commonly ascribed to it in connection with the invocation of Jesus as Lord, it could not be otherwise; for it is at one and the same time the *testimonium* for his lordship and for his session at God's right hand. True, the *testimonium* also points on to the consummation, "till I make your enemies your footstool"— but in the New Testament it is frequently quoted without that addendum, and in the places where the addendum is quoted, only once is it expounded (1 Cor. 15:25–28). The perspective of the language about the session at God's right hand in confessional formulae is regularly that of Jesus' present intercessory ministry (cf. Rom. 8:34).

It cannot be proved—it cannot even be rendered probable— that at first this present ministry of the exalted Christ was not envisaged. Stephen's vision of the Son of Man standing at God's right hand (Acts 7:55-56) comes indeed in a Hellenistic section of Acts, but the title "Son of man" (here only in the New Testament occurring outside the Gospels) is strikingly un-Hellenistic. Moreover, Stephen's words chime in impressively with the dominical logion of Luke 12:8, "every one who acknowledges me before men, the Son of man also will acknowledge before the angels of God"—a logion with peculiar claims to be recognized as an *ipsissimum verbum Christi*.

The ascription of an intercessory ministry to the one seated at God's right hand may, if Old Testament *testimonia* are sought for it, go back to a combination of Isaiah 53:12 with Psalm 110:1 and Daniel 7:13—a combination so primitive that an original setting in the context of Jesus' earthly ministry cannot be excluded.

Those who envisage a shift from the earlier association of Jesus' lordship with his coming parousia to its later association with his present exaltation find motivation for the shift in the delay of the parousia. But a large question mark should be set against the whole supposition that the delay in the parousia caused a major change in early Christian perspective. That it constituted a problem is plain; but some of the leaders of apostolic Christianity appear to have taken the problem in their stride, realizing that the "when" of the parousia was its least important feature. We can trace the progression of Paul's thought in this regard from the earliest to the latest of his undisputed writings. For him the realization increased as time went on that his death before the parousia was more probable than was his survival until it took place; but, far from making him recast the main lines of his thought, this realization enabled him to explore and expound essential Paulinism at a deeper level than before.

In short, it seems impossible on the available evidence to accept the view that the association of Jesus' lordship with his present exaltation and the idea of his exercising an intercessory ministry at God's right hand resulted from the delay in the parousia. Both are attested too early in the first Christian generation to be plausibly accounted for in this way.

IV

It is quite improbable that Christian usage was influenced materially by the practice of calling the Roman Emperor κύριος (Latin *dominus*) in a sense that connoted divinity, for the Christian usage was too well established by the time κύριος or *dominus* came to be generally employed as an imperial title with divine connotation.

Gaius, as we know, demanded divine honors during his brief principate (A.D. 37–41), but his precedent was not regarded as auspicious. In Egypt and the East the emperor inherited the designation κύριος from the Ptolemies and other Hellenistic dynasts; from the time of Nero onward, Deissmann marks a notable increase of such ascriptions.[7] According to Dio Cassius,[8] Tiridates of Armenia hailed Nero as his δεσπότης and θεός—but that was oriental *Hofstil*. The reference to Nero as ὁ κύριος by Festus in Acts 25:26 is a form of courtesy, like "His Majesty" today. Domitian is noteworthy for his predilection for being addressed or referred to as *dominus et deus noster*,[9] but while that may be relevant to the "name of blasphemy" borne by the imperial beast of Revelation 13:1, it is too late to have provided a model for Christians to follow in their language about Jesus.

Naturally, when Christians were confronted with claims such as Domitian's, they refused to acknowledge them, for in this sense they knew but one κύριος, Jesus, even as they knew but one θεός, the Father (1 Cor. 8:6). So when, several decades after the end of the apostolic age, Polycarp was asked, "What harm is there in saying κύριος Καῖσαρ, and offering sacrifice and so forth, and so saving your life?", there was but one answer he could give.[10] But while the confession κύριος Ἰησοῦς involved a head-on clash with the formula κύριος Καῖσαρ when they confronted each other, they arose independently.

It is equally improbable that the wording κύριος Ἰησοῦς was influenced by such usage as κύριος Σάραπις in the mystery and similar cults. Paul, in affirming that for Christians there is one κύριος, recognizes that in the world of his day there are κύριοι πολλοί (1 Cor. 8:5), but he does not suggest that Jesus is κύριος by analogy with them. In any case, the title κύριος appears less frequently as the predicate of a cult-divinity than is popularly supposed, and where it does so appear (as in Egypt and Syria by contrast, for example, with Asia Minor), it appears as one title among many, without the pre-eminence which attaches to it in Christian usage.[11]

V

Māranā-thā ("Our Lord, come!"), which appears in the *Didache* as a eucharistic invocation,[12] was in all probability used in the early Palestinian Aramaic-speaking communities in a eucharistic context; otherwise it would be hard to account for its appearance in such a context in a Greek church order. It cannot indeed be proved that its one New Testament occurrence (1 Cor. 16:22) is, as Lietzmann suggested,[13] part of a quotation from a liturgical sequence, thus:

> Versicle: If any one does not love the Lord, let him be anathema.
> Response: *Māranā-thā!*
> Versicle: The grace of the Lord Jesus be with you.

But the occurrence of the Greek form of the invocation at the end of the Apocalypse (Rev. 22:20) comes in such a responsive setting, and in a book which in its language, and especially in its hymnody, has been manifestly influenced by Christian liturgical usage. We may reflect, moreover, that the Apocalypse, although we have it in a Greek text, is not generally regarded as a notably Hellenistic work.

In any case, the invocation is most appropriate to a eucharistic setting. At the Last Supper, Jesus looked forward to his reunion with his disciples in the kingdom of God, and his instruction that they should break bread as his memorial charges them to anticipate, if not to hasten, his parousia. Paul puts this idea in his own words when he says that the eating of the bread and drinking from the cup constitute a proclamation of the Lord's death till he comes (1 Cor. 11:26). In the Eucharist the partition between now and then, between "already" and "not yet," between the disciples' present condition and the coming parousia, wore very thin. As Jesus had made himself known to the two at Emmaus in the breaking of bread, so the disciples continued to pray especially at the Eucharist that they might now see him in their midst, as disciples still do when they sing:

"To every faithful soul appear
And show Thy real presence here!"

But in what sense is Jesus called *mar* or *māranā* in this Aramaic invocation? Certainly in much more than a courtesy sense: "Come, sir" or "Come, rabbi" is out of the question. In the eucharistic setting a connotation approaching divinity is implied: "Our Lord, come!" is the only adequate rendering. And if indeed the setting of the invocation is eucharistic, it is the eucharistic setting of the early Palestinian church. Whatever difficulties scholars may find in the way of accepting this, they are trifling compared with the difficulties attending any other account of the matter—such as that the language is that of the bilingual Christian community in or around Syrian Antioch or Damascus or that the invocation has the form of an oath sworn to God and is not addressed to Christ.[14] *Māranā-thā* is a testimony to the place which the exalted and expected Christ had in the worship of the most primitive church.

VI

The most impressive evidence of the superlative connotation which κύριος carried as a designation of Jesus is the free application to Jesus in the New Testament of Septuagint quotations referring to the God of Israel (where κύριος is the rendering of YHWH). This practice is not confined to one author or to one school of thought.

In John 12:38, for example, Isaiah 53:1 is quoted in the Septuagint version with the prefixed κύριε—"Lord, who has believed our message, and to whom has the arm of the Lord been bared?"— as a prophecy of the unbelief of Jesus' contemporaries (cf. Rom. 10:16). But then this unbelief is explained in terms of the familiar *testimonium* in Isaiah 6:9–10 (cf. Mark 4:12 and parallels; Acts 28:26–27), and the Evangelist concludes: "Isaiah said this because he saw his glory and spoke of him"—an echo, perhaps, of a targumic version of Isaiah 6:1 ("I saw the glory of the Lord"). The implication is that the thrice-holy one whom Isaiah saw in the temple was Jesus, and even possibly that the Lord (Hebrew YHWH) whose arm is bared (Isaiah 53:1) is Jesus.

However this may be, there is no dubiety when we come to Paul. For him the Old Testament "day of YHWH" becomes not only (as in the Septuagint) ἡμέρα κυρίου but ἡμέρα χριστοῦ or ἡμέρα τοῦ κυρίου (ἡμῶν) Ἰησοῦ (χριστοῦ). The assurance of salvation to anyone who confesses Jesus as Lord, already quoted from Romans 10:9, is buttressed by the promise of Joel 2:32, that whoever invokes the name of the Lord (Hebrew YHWH) will be saved (Rom. 10:13).

In 1 Peter 3:14–15 there is an unmistakable quotation from Isaiah 8:12–13, but in place of "YHWH your God, him shall you sanctify," the New Testament text has "sanctify in your hearts the Christ as Lord."

In Hebrews 1:10 the Septuagint version of Psalm 102:25— "Of old, Lord, thou hast founded the earth . . ."—is taken as addressed to Christ; even if the vocative κύριε of the Septuagint has no counterpart in the Hebrew, the whole psalm in Hebrew is addressed to YHWH (if the Septuagint implies a change of speaker from verse 23 onward, the writer to the Hebrews understands the change to mean that the Father is now addressing the Son—and calling him κύριε).

Whatever the Semitic original of κύριος may have been in 1 Enoch 1:9, quoted in Jude 14–15 (and indeed whether there was any counterpart to κύριος in the Semitic text or not), the one whose coming with his holy myriads is announced in First Enoch is as certainly the God of Israel as Jude takes him to be the κύριος of the Christians.

As for the Apocalypse, the designation of Jesus as "King of kings and Lord of lords" (Rev. 19:16) or "Lord of lords and King of kings" (Rev. 17:14) echoes Deuteronomy 10:17, "YHWH your God is . . . Lord of lords" or Daniel 2:47, where Nebuchadnezzar acknowledges that Daniel's God is "God of gods and Lord of kings"—but there is nothing surprising about this in a book which can take the attributes of the Ancient of Days as he is portrayed in Daniel 7:9 and ascribe them to the "one like a son of man" (Rev. 1:13–14).

The opening oracle of Psalm 110 is one of the earliest Christian *testimonia*. The motif of Jesus as the exalted Messiah sitting at God's right hand, common to several strains of primitive Christianity, is regularly expressed in language drawn from this *testimonium*. The introductory words, εἶπεν κύριος τῷ κυρίῳ μου, though frequently omitted, are usually implied. They are quoted in Acts 2:34, where they provide the basis for the following affirmation that "God has made him both κύριος and Messiah, this Jesus whom you crucified." They are quoted also, as the essential point of the quotation, in Mark 12:35–37 and parallels, where the question is asked how the Messiah, commonly believed to be the son of David, could be referred to by David as his κύριος.

That the person addressed in the oracle of Psalm 110:1 is Messiah was generally accepted by Jewish exegetes of the time and, in their turn, by Christians. But Christians from earliest days believed as firmly as the "scribes" did that the Messiah (by them identified with Jesus) was son of David (cf. Rom. 1:3); the problem posed by Jesus would thus be a problem for them too. Quite soon they learned to think of it as a problem with a simple solution, when the doctrine of Jesus' divine preexistence was accepted, but in the earliest stages of the gospel tradition the question as framed by Jesus must have seemed to be (superficially, at any rate) a contradiction of their belief that Jesus, being by birth son of David, was already in the messianic succession. The incident may thus be regarded, according to reductionist form-critical methodology, as having on this ground a claim to authenticity.

Another allusion to the same passage comes later in the Synoptic narrative, where Jesus at his trial says to the high priest, "You will see the Son of man sitting at the right hand of Power" (Mark 14:62)—or, in the Lukan form, "From now on the Son of man shall be seated at the right hand of the power of God" (Luke 22:69). These words contribute to the construction of blasphemy placed by the Sanhedrin on Jesus' reply of which they are a part, and this may point to a belief in some quarters that the person addressed in the oracle was of more than human stature.

It is readily intelligible that the Septuagint version of Psalm 110:1 could have facilitated the practice of ascribing to Jesus Old Testament passages where κύριος renders YHWH. For in the Septuagint here there is no distinction between the rendering of YHWH and the rendering of 'ādōn; κύριος is used as equivalent of both.[15] But if Septuagint usage *facilitated* the practice, it cannot fully account for it. So far as Psalm 110 is concerned, consideration must be given to the fact that the person whom the psalmist calls "my κύριος" is invited by the God of Israel, who is also the God of heaven, to sit at his right hand; whatever of subordination this implies, it implies at the same time exaltation—exaltation to be Lord of the universe as well as Lord of the believing community.

The ascription to a man of Old Testament passages relating to the God of Israel would be incredible on the part of any Jew, "Hebrew" or Hellenist, did we not have New Testament evidence for their early and pervasive ascription to Jesus. It can be accounted for only by the immediate impact which personal confrontation with Jesus—living, crucified, risen and exalted—made on his followers. The verbal coincidence in the Greek Bible of κύριος as the rendering of YHWH and κύριος as the rendering of 'ādōn would not have been sufficient in itself to make them take a course which they would normally have felt by instinct to be blasphemous. It was because of nothing but the personal impact of Jesus in their experience that language which they would have repudiated as blasphemous if applied to anyone else appeared to be the most natural language in the world when applied spontaneously to him.

Of all the Old Testament passages with YHWH as subject which the New Testament refers to Jesus, none is more interesting than Philippians 2:9–11, at which we have already looked. I need not recapitulate the arguments for regarding the passage to which these verses belong as pre-Pauline.[16] The "name above every name" bestowed by God on Jesus is almost certainly κύριος in the sense of YHWH, and the affirmation that "Jesus Christ is κύριος" means, practically, that Jesus Christ is YHWH. The Old Testament passage here alluded to is Isaiah 45:22–23, where YHWH, proclaiming, "I am God, and there is no other," goes on: "By myself I have sworn, from my mouth has gone forth in righteousness a word that shall not return: 'To me every knee shall bow, every tongue shall swear.' " We should note, moreover, that this comes from a section of Old Testament prophecy where the exclusive power and glory of YHWH as the only God are repeatedly underlined. "I am YHWH, and there is no other, besides me there is no God" (Isa. 45:5; cf. 44:6, 8; 45:21). "I, I am YHWH, and besides me there is no savior" (Isa. 43:11). "I am YHWH, that is my name; my glory I give to no other" (Isa. 42:8).

But in this early Christian hymn, to be dated well within the first Christian generation, the supreme name is bestowed on Jesus, the glory of the only God is shared with Jesus, and is not diminished but enhanced in the process—for when every tongue confesses that Jesus Christ is Lord, this is done "to the glory of God the Father." No angel or man, it is implied, by any act or word, can exalt Jesus so highly as God has already done.

It is a joy and a privilege to take part in this token of honour to Dr. William Childs Robinson. Among many good reasons for gladly accepting the invitation to contribute to this complimentary volume, one may be mentioned: the editor of *The Evangelical Quarterly* thinks with gratitude and appreciation of the help and encouragement which Dr. Robinson has given for over twenty years as Editorial Correspondent to this as to so many other enterprises in the field of biblical and historical theology. May his bow abide in strength!

III

PAUL'S UNDERSTANDING OF RIGHTEOUSNESS
Bo Reicke

Many experts of theology can tell us that Paul rejected some old ideas of a righteousness based on the works of the law, and preached a new sort of justification by faith alone. But few realize that misunderstanding arises if an abstract doctrine without relation to concrete life is created. The following lines are intended to discuss a traditional view often taken over by modern expositions and investigations. That view implies that Paul was eager to introduce a new doctrine or at least that he endeavored to develop or to purify current theologumena. He is, for instance, supposed to have made great progress by replacing the legalistic with a forensic conception of God's righteousness.

I

As a theological expression, the Latin word *justificatio* is common since Augustine and Jerome. Paul uses the corresponding Greek noun δικαίωσις in Romans 4:25 and 5:18, but these are the only places where the noun occurs in the New Testament. More characteristic of the New Testament and its concrete way of thinking is the adjective δίκαιος, "righteous," which is often found in the Gospels (33 times) and in the Pauline Epistles (17 times). Its substantivized equivalent δικαιοσύνη, "righteousness," is frequently used by Paul and his collaborators (57 times). The corresponding verb δικαιόω, "to justify," is also typical of the Pauline Epistles (27 instances, as against 12 in other New Testament writings).

In the New Testament, accordingly, there is no elaborate doctrine of "justification." One can only study the adjective δίκαιος, the verb δικαιόω, and the context in which they illustrate Paul's dramatic representation of God's and man's righteousness.

Elementary information will be afforded by a semantic analysis. Since δίκη is related to δείκνυμι, "to show,"[1] its fundamental meaning is "directive, order, pattern" (*Iliad*, xvi. 542, "judgment"; *Odyssey*, iv. 691, "disposition"). Therefore δίκαιος essentially means "being in order," whether the order in question is understood to be a prescription, a principle, or a pattern (*Iliad*, xi. 832, "respectable"; *Odyssey*, xiii. 201, "civilized"). A quite unsophisticated meaning is often found, as in the phrase "to make a horse δίκαιος" in the sense of training it for riding (Xenophon, Mem. iv., 4, 5).

The words δίκη (or δικαιοσύνη) and δίκαιος are used in the Greek Bible and by Paul to render the Hebrew words ṣedeq and ṣaddīq. In fact, ṣedeq also has such a simple fundamental meaning: that which is in order (Deut. 25:15, "a correct weight"). Thus ṣaddīq can sometimes be used for "correct" in quite a general sense (Isaiah 41:26, "He is right," as having foretold something correctly).

On the whole, etymological observations illustrate the fact that δίκαιος and related words are not used to indicate any isolated quality such as blond or pale, but always imply a relation to some criterion. In a phrase like "this is the right sort of bread," average man establishes that criterion. Such a *homo mensura* principle is generally behind the popular use of δίκη and δίκαιος in Greek literature. In this respect the Bible takes a different attitude, for here the criterion is more often God than man. When somebody is said to be ṣaddīq or δίκαιος, it is generally meant that he is acceptable in the eyes of God (Gen. 6:9; 18:23–28; Isa. 3:10; 53:11; Hab. 2:4; Matt. 1:19, etc.; Mark 2:17; 6:20; Luke 1:6, etc.; Acts 3:14, etc.).

The characteristic inclination of Old Testament writers to concentrate attention on the attitude, decision, or judgment of God led to repeated confessions of his eminent, unique, even absolute blamelessness and righteousness (Exod. 9:27; Deut. 32:4; Isa. 45:21; Jer. 12:1; Zeph. 3:5; Pss. 7:9, 11; 11:7; 112:4, etc.). In pietistic Judaism, the conclusion was drawn that God alone possesses righteousness (1QH i. 26, iv. 31, xvii. 20), though in his grace he permits the convert to participate in it (1QS xi. 3, 5, 12-14). God is here the criterion of his own righteousness, which is therefore understood as integrity, perfection, and supremacy.

II

Paul based his central preaching on this Jewish conviction of God's supreme righteousness. In well-known contexts he spoke emphatically of righteousness as a gift coming from God in Christ, given in faith to men: Galatians 2:16; Romans 1:17 (δικιαοσύνη θεοῦ, genitive of origin as in Rom. 1:1, 16; 10:3; 15:16; cf. ἐκ θεοῦ in Phil. 3:9). He never dreamed of representing this as a new doctrine or a personal contribution, as modern scholars regard it. The apostle was convinced that God had revealed himself to Abraham, Moses, and the Prophets. Christ fulfilled the promise they had received. Paul and the other apostles were called to preach this common gospel (Rom. 1:2; 3:21; 4:11–12; 15:20).

(a) It is certainly remarkable that another terminology is found in the earliest epistles of Paul preserved in the canon, that is, in his letters to the Thessalonians written around A.D. 52 and 53. Here the effect of the gospel is not yet said to be righteousness, but participation in the Holy Spirit and holiness (1 Thess. 1:5-6; 3:13; 4:8), an experience which Paul repeatedly characterizes as sanctification (1 Thess. 3:13; 4:3-4, 7; 2 Thess. 2:13). A reference to the righteousness of God is made only in connection with the future judgment (2 Thess. 1:5-7). Paul found it natural to speak of holiness in correspondence with Christians coming mainly from a Gentile environment (1 Thess. 1:9), whereas the conception of righteousness appeared more suitable for readers of Jewish background.

(b) Shortly afterward, Paul thought it necessary to specify his view on man's justification in his epistle to the Galatians, which may be dated to about A.D. 55 and was written mainly for Christians with a Jewish background or inclinations to Jewish thinking. The reason he took up the problem was his shocking experience in Antioch, where he found Peter and some leading Jewish Christians no longer following the decision of the Apostolic Council of A.D. 49 to accept Gentile Christians as full members of the church (Gal. 2:11-13).

In this dialectic situation Paul referred to his own gospel and his personal preaching as based on revelation (Gal. 1:11-12, 16; 2:2). But he did not think for a moment that he had discovered or invented this gospel, though ancient Marcionism and modern ultra-Paulinism both imply that he was such an innovator. On the contrary, Paul emphasized that there is no other gospel (Gal. 1:7).

He was firmly convinced that God had revealed the same gospel of belief to Abraham (Gal. 3:8), Moses (3:10), the Prophets (3:11), and later to Peter and other apostles as well as to Paul himself (2:7), although their missionary fields were to be divided. For the apostle Paul there was one truth only, and because of the pre-established harmony of revelation this same truth had been given to all elect people, especially the apostles. The attitude taken by Peter and the others in Antioch did not mean that they diverged from any new theology invented by Paul, but that they no longer stood by the common truth of the gospel (Gal. 2:14), a truth which Peter was said to know very well (2:16). In other contexts, Paul expressed the same conviction—that his gospel was nothing but that holy tradition represented by Moses and the Prophets (Rom. 1:2; 3:21), Jesus and the apostles (1 Cor. 7:10; 15:5-8). Even if he underlined his independence of human authorities (Gal. 1:12), he also quoted common traditions in his teaching (1 Cor. 11:23; 15:3) and was grateful for an exchange of spiritual gifts (Rom. 1:11-14). Paul never claimed to be a constructive theologian or to have replaced, improved, and purified older religious conceptions, but only to have preserved the authentic Old and New Testament tradition. This is especially characteristic of his comments on God's righteousness in Christ and in faith (e.g., Rom. 10:4, 8).

But why did Paul not accept the view taken by those who found the works of the law essential, and therefore started this discussion with Peter in Antioch (Gal. 2:14-16)? His concern was for the justification and salvation of the Gentiles (Gal. 3:8, 14, 28; cf. Rom. 1:16; 2:10; 3:29). He was not dominated by any theological ambitions, but only by missionary interests.

Paul did not regard this universalistic interpretation of the gospel as his invention, but rather as the result of his confrontation with Christ (Gal. 1:16), and for the apostle this was the only personal factor involved. Yet it did not exclude that pre-established harmony of tradition referred to previously. He probably would have been very depressed if somebody had told him that scholars of the nineteenth and twentieth centuries were going to ascribe to him such a great innovation as the doctrine of justification is said to be. Paul represented himself as being the last as well as the least of the apostles to whom Christ had revealed himself (1 Cor. 15:8-9).

Paul's firm conviction of being only an instrument of holy revelation and traditions is overlooked by many scholars whose great ambition is to establish the development and to define the importance of Paul's new insights.

An evolution of ideas must be assumed to have taken place in early Christianity, and men like Peter, James, and Paul certainly did not have the same mind or use the same terms. However, it is unrealistic to believe that exact separation of pre-Pauline and Pauline elements in Paul's epistles is possible. With the exception of clear quotations, no independent documents illustrate precisely which traditions Paul used, beyond a general assumption that preaching, prayers, prophecy, baptism, the Eucharist, catechism, and other church activities inspired him. Neither can anybody know exactly how much he changed this material. All reconstructions based upon analysis of his sayings will necessarily be a priori statements and depend on the scholar's personal taste. Today the result is also endless disagreement about verses and half-verses, if not mere reproduction of what some renowned scholar has already written about their authenticity or non-authenticity. Rejection of this modern scholasticism does not mean conservative fundamentalism but historical criticism, for regard must be paid to what the documents really tell us and do not tell us. Paul, who claimed to represent authentic revelation and tradition, would have been quite happy to admit that not only his express quotations, but also practically everything he wrote or dictated had a pre-Pauline origin. At the same time any reflection based on common sense will make it clear that if Paul took over much traditional material, he used it consciously for his special purposes and gave it a meaning in the present context. Students of the Bible will also know that

Paul was intelligent enough to reject mechanical repetition of phrases without the collaboration of reason, and that he criticized meaningless language as barbarous nonsense (1 Cor. 14:9-19). The current method of higher criticism is less critical.

Such objections must be raised against recent discussions of Paul's contributions to what is called the doctrine of justification, because higher criticism is especially misused in this connection. The argumentation of Galatians and other epistles implies rather that Paul did not think he developed any new conception of justification, but faithfully preserved the gospel as it was revealed in the Old and New Covenants. He may have given himself too little credit, but only the angels know to what extent. At any rate, his conviction of being an honest reproducer of given traditions is a historical factor more important than any modern construction of a logical development.

III

Consequently, when Paul discussed the righteousness of God and man with such intensity and enthusiasm in his Epistle to the Romans, he was not proud of having invented a new theological system as a modern professor might be.

(a) If it was not for subjective reasons, however, why did Paul make God's righteousness the main topic of Romans?

A common suggestion implies that Paul had to struggle with the problem of the law, and therefore was led to analyze the conception of righteousness, understood substantially in a forensic sense. Now if this were true, there would have been a discussion of the law in the first chapter. Instead, the righteousness announced by the gospel is the starting point of the exposition (Rom. 1:16-17). The whole argumentation in Romans proceeds from the gospel to the law. Each time beginning with God's righteousness (1:17; 3:5-6, 21; 10:3), Paul discusses the law in the light of this principle (2:12; 3:19, 31; 10:4, *et passim*).

It is the chance of salvation not only for Israel but also for the Gentiles which dominates the main sections of Romans treating God's righteousness: 1:16-17; 3:21-31; and 10:1-13. (The Gentiles are mentioned in 1:16; 3:29; and 10:12, the latter passage being a central point within the broad discussion of the problem in 9:1—11:36.) There the law is only a secondary and partial aspect. Paul did not write in order to discuss theoretical difficulties but to promote a practical enterprise, his missionary activity.

Romans therefore deals with God's righteousness in the sense of that absolute fairness with which God is willing to save the faithful. In the gospel God gives Israel and the Gentiles the same chances of salvation (1:16). God's wrath against sinful mankind as well as his grace toward all believers is the same in relation to Jews and Greeks, for with him there is no partiality (2:4-11). But his wrath is only a secondary aspect of his righteousness; the primary one is his grace revealed in Christ for the believers (3:22). This was the starting point of Paul's considerations on God's righteousness when he wrote to Rome as the apostle to the Gentiles (11:13).

(b) Quoting the Old Testament, Paul was firmly convinced that man's righteousness is not based on any natural talent and cannot be achieved by any personal efforts (Rom. 3:10-20). One can only receive it as a gift of God conveyed by Christ (3:24). A clear definition is found in a central passage of Romans: "[He appointed Christ to be an instrument of reconciliation] . . . in order to demonstrate his righteousness in the present time, so that he should be righteous and justify everyone governed by faith in Jesus" (3:26). The point is that man cannot establish any personal righteousness—as the Jewish moralists thought (10:3)—but is offered participation in righteousness by faith in Christ, the perfect revelation of God's righteousness (3:21-22).

Seeing in Christ the source of all righteousness is characteristic of Paul's thinking. Christ is God's own wisdom, righteousness, holiness, and salvation (1 Cor. 1:30), and in him the believers are made (manifestations of) God's righteousness (2 Cor. 5:18-21). He is furthermore the fulfillment of the righteousness announced by the law (Rom. 10:4), and to find him in his Word is to gain that righteousness (10:5-8).

When speaking of justification by faith, one should not overlook the fact that Paul ascribes such a central function to Christ.

Theology has generally been more interested to find out details
about the situation or development of the human subject. Re-
moval of attention from christology to anthropology has led the
discussion into a serious dilemma.

Protestant theology has often been inclined to define justification as a forensic act, a judgment or declaration by which God
treats man as if he were blameless although he is a sinner. In
this context, man is supposed to stand before God without any
good works, but nevertheless his faith is regarded as a meritorious
attitude which gives him a license here or in heaven—modern
theology prefers abstract expressions such as eschatological. The
result will easily be a new form of legalism—just what Paul
rejected when he spoke of "grace alone." Catholic theology has
generally preferred to describe justification as being a process by
which the economy of God is accompanied on the human level,
and which includes at least some change and some efforts of the
human subject. This process is further analyzed, and is characterized by such expressions as habitus, infusion, inherence, and so
on. It will not be unfair to say that here the result is often a
thinking in terms of metaphysic transubstantiation and moral
collaboration, which are difficult to harmonize with Paul when he
treats Christ's righteousness as being effective directly and by
"faith alone."

Certainly both positions are based on real concern for the
biblical message and the salvation of mankind. But they cannot
be reconciled by any simple combination.[2]

Would it not be helpful to raise the eyes from this level of
man to the level of God and Christ? Paul speaks of justification
in connection with salvation history and christology, not as part
of any detailed anthropology.

We should observe the theological context in which the noun
"justification" ($\delta\iota\kappa\alpha\iota\omega\sigma\iota\varsigma$) is used when it appears in Romans
4:25 and 5:18, the only passages of the New Testament where this
noun is found.

Romans 4:25 is the conclusion of the apostle's comments on
Abraham's faith as described in Genesis 15:6: "Abraham believed in the Lord [LXX: in God], and he counted it to him

for righteousness." This passage is quoted or reference is made to it several times (as earlier in Galatians 3:6, now in Romans 4:3, 9, 22). Paul was eager to show in what sense Abraham was the father of the elect people. By his faith and righteousness Abraham served independently of the law as a prototype for believers of all nations (Gal. 3:7; Rom. 4:17, 23-24). Paul gave Genesis 15:6 quite a particular meaning in the framework of salvation history. He wanted to base his interpretation neither on the current Jewish exegesis of the passage, nor on any isolated analysis of it, but on his understanding of its principal importance within the divine economy. In order to realize exactly what Paul meant when he quoted Genesis 15:6 in Romans 4:3, one must leave out all other theological and philological considerations and pay regard only to the immediate context and the general relation between Abraham and the believers.

The starting point is what Scripture says Abraham "found" or experienced (Rom. 4:1, $εὑρηκέναι$). By using this verb, Paul may have thought of an Old Testament phrase like "Noah found grace" (Gen. 6:8). In any case, Abraham did not produce anything, but only received the experience in question when he was elected. He did not contribute to it by any right activity or reaction, for this would have given him a merit before God (Rom. 4:2), which is not compatible with the principle of God's absolute supremacy (cf. 1 Cor. 1:29). The apostle's critical remarks on the idea of merit and reward were evidently directed against Jewish inclinations to see a merit in the patriarch's belief (1 Macc. 2:51 f., glory ascribed to Abraham because he "was found faithful"; Sir. 44:19, "nobody found like Abraham in glory" because he kept the Law; Phil. Abr. 262, the patriarch is praised by Moses because "he believed God," and faith is "confirmed by work"). Paul took another position by emphasizing that Abraham was justified without any work and merit.

Therefore it is not fair to let the apostle think in terms of merits again when he quotes the Genesis reference to Abraham's faith (Rom. 4:3). Even if faith is no work, any justification which is the remuneration of a suitable attitude must imply the acknowledgment of some merit. The interpretation Paul gave

Genesis 15:6 must be understood in such a way that his desire to avoid the idea of merit is taken seriously.

Just after the quotation of Genesis 15:6 in Romans 4:3, Paul gives his special interpretation of the passage in verses 4–6, saying that faith and pay are "reckoned" from different points of view— faith as a grace, pay as a debt. The comparison implies that several elements are common, though a transaction resulting from grace has another background than one resulting from debt. One of these common elements is exactly the verb "to be reckoned" ($\dot{\epsilon}\lambda o\gamma\iota\sigma\theta\eta$, $\lambda o\gamma\dot{\iota}\zeta\epsilon\tau\alpha\iota$). First it relates to Abraham's faith, then to a working-man's pay. Unless the comparison is reduced to a careless play upon words, the reader has to suppose that Paul really meant this verb to have corresponding meanings in both cases. Since a working-man's pay is "reckoned" to him in the sense of being assigned to him (cf. 2 Sam. 4:2, "was attributed to"), Paul obviously understood the Genesis passage to say that Abraham's faith had been assigned to him by God as a dispensation of grace. For the logical structure of the contraposition is simply this:

Abraham's faith was assigned to him for the purpose of righteousness (4:3).
Whereas a workingman's pay is assigned to him as a *debt* (4:4), the elect one's faith is assigned to him for the purpose of righteousness (4:5) as a *grace* (a special endowment) or a blessing (4:6).

The parallelism does not make any sense until assignment or dispensation is understood to be such a *tertium comparationis*. In this way only the actual difference comes into sight: the reason for the assignment is here grace, and there debt. God is not supposed to pay any debt, but to bestow his supreme grace on a man whom he elects. The latter is allowed to believe, and thus to be saved from an ungodly environment. Belief is no achievement or decision of this man, to be accepted by God instead of moral efforts, but an experience spontaneously given to him by God, to enable him to let the energy of God's righteousness work on him (Rom. 1:16). If faith were not regarded as such a free gift, it would not be quite honest of Paul to state that every merit is excluded (3:27), or that Abraham was justified without any merit (4:2) and by grace alone, whereas a workingman is paid for his achievements (4:4). Paul's consistently theocentric idea of election also implies that God is the initiator of man's belief (Gal. 1:5, "set apart and called through his grace"; Rom. 8:28, "called according to his decision"; 12:3, "corresponding to the portion of faith that God has allotted him"). Like the corresponding Hebrew verb (*ḥāshab*), the Greek verb in question (λογίζομαι) is rather seldom used by the Septuagint and the New Testament for counting, but more often for thinking, and this is quite in harmony with our references to God's dispensations for his chosen people.

Abraham was not declared righteous in a fictive forensic sense, but was made righteous (Rom. 4:2, ἐδικαιώθη). His belief led to righteousness (4:3, εἰς δικαιοσύνην), because it opened his mind for the activity of the One who makes a godless man righteous (4:5). Afterward his righteousness was confirmed by the seal of circumcision (4:11). This reality of his righteousness made it a guarantee for believers of all nations, to whom righteousness based on faith would be assigned (4:12). Abraham's belief further opened his mind for the activity of the One who makes the dead alive (4:17), which he was allowed to experience when the promise of a descendant was fulfilled in spite of his age (4:18–21). For this reason, too, faith "was assigned to him for the purpose of righteousness" (4:22), so that Abraham should be a father and model of all who believe in a resurrection from death.

The exposition is completely oriented toward the justification of the Christian believers: this Scripture (Gen. 15:6) was written for us (Rom. 4:23–24a). Just as belief in the God who raises man from death was assigned to Abraham (4:22–23), so faith was to be assigned to all those who believe now in the One who has raised Christ from death (4:24b). This typology implies more than a mere similarity, for Abraham is the father of God's people.

How fundamental God's dispensation of grace was for Paul is also evident from his concluding remarks on justification in Romans 4:25: Christ was sacrificed and "raised [from the dead] for our justification." A provisional judgment, including only a fictive acknowledgment of each sinner for the purpose of being made righteous when the end comes, is not compatible with the universal efficacy which Paul ascribed to Christ's sacrifice and victory (cf. Rom. 3:24, "justified through the redemption found in Christ"; 6:2 and 7, "dead from sin, justified from sin"). Thus the justification offered in Christ is not forensic, but dynamic (1:16, "power"; 4:21, "mighty").

Certainly the individual believer is neither supposed to be perfect once for all, nor to have acquired some metaphysic substance on the basis of which he should develop perfection. Paul made the believer's righteousness refer expressly to Christ's dominion: "Jesus our *Lord*, who was . . . raised for our justification" (4:24-25). Christ's royal power is what makes it possible that former sinners are now the servants of righteousness (6:18). Because they are the descendants of Abraham (4:16) and confessors of the risen Lord (4:24), they participate in a dynamic, collective righteousness which is no mere fiction, but real freedom (6:7).

The second passage mentioned earlier, Romans 5:18, belongs to a context which makes it even more evident that Paul's conception of justification was collective, not atomistic. Just as sinful mankind is collectively the object of God's wrath (1:18), so those who have now been justified by faith have all together peace with God (5:1). The infusion of God's love (5:5) is not a ground of further justification, but a sign of its present reality, as was earlier the seal which Abraham received (4:11). Paul was therefore able to conclude that all those who have now been justified in Christ's blood will much more be saved from the wrath (5:9). He certainly thought of a collective experience. Furthermore, just as one man's (Adam's) transgression led to sin, death, and condemnation for all mankind (5:12, 18a), so one man's (Christ's) righteousness brought about a justification implying life for all people (5:18b). Attention is not paid to stages in the development of the soul, but to events of importance for the world. Paul takes up the idea of a dominion (cf. "our Lord" in 4:24), this time expressly mentioning the royal power of sin on the one hand, and of grace and the receivers of righteousness on the other (5:14, 17, 21). Righteousness is understood as the result of being dominated by grace within the kingdom of God and his Christ. The way of thinking is not forensic, but dynamic and collective. Romans 5:18 speaks of justification in a context which is primarily referred to salvation history and christology, and not so pronouncedly to individual anthropology.

Of course it would be wrong to say that Paul was not concerned with the application of justification, sanctification, and salvation to individuals. Righteousness appeared to him as something already established in Christ, but the apostle's most burning desire was that its power should be active on each man. By understanding righteousness in a dynamic sense and with reference to the royal power of Christ, however, one is able to avoid the dilemma between a purely objective or a purely subjective conception of righteousness.[3]

Nevertheless there is still a problem. Why did the apostle use the noun "justification" only in Romans 4:25 and 5:18, in contexts which show his interest concentrated on the universal basis of the new righteousness, whereas he does not seem greatly concerned here with its personal application? And why did Paul occupy himself so much here with Abraham and the first and second Adam, why did he speak of "all people" with such emphasis (4:11, 16 bis; 5:12, 18)? The answer is easy, if the apostle's main concern is not forgotten: the conversion and salvation of Israel and the Gentiles. As the missionary to the Gentiles, he was eager to point out that righteousness is now offered to all nations independently of the law, as a gift of "grace alone" to be received in faith. The proclamation of that righteousness in an objective way, *extra nos,* was a vital part of his missionary program (e.g., 3:21, "now the righteousness of God has been manifested"). Paul kept the same missionary concern foremost in his attention when he discussed the possession of righteousness by "faith alone": All nations should, apart from any works of the law and only because of their faith in Christ, be allowed to join the church (5:1-2, "justified by faith . . . we have access [in faith] into this grace wherein we stand"). Only in this practical, missionary context—in connection with a believer's admission to Christian fellowship and to baptism—did Paul understand righteousness forensically.

IV

PAUL AND THE LAW
George Eldon Ladd

Paul's thought about the law is difficult to understand because he seems to make numerous contradictory statements. He asserts that those who do the law shall be justified (Rom. 2:13) and shall find life by the law (Rom. 10:5; Gal. 3:12); but at the same time he affirms that no man shall be justified by the law (Rom. 3:20) but is only brought to death by the written code of the law (2 Cor. 3:6) for the law cannot give life (Gal. 3:21). He claims himself to have been blameless in his obedience to the law (Phil. 3:6) and yet asserts that no man can perfectly submit to the law (Rom. 3:20).

Paul's teaching about the law is often approached from the perspective of the historical experience either of Paul himself as a Jewish rabbi, or of a typical first-century Jew under the law. However, Paul's thought must be seen neither as a confession of his spiritual autobiography, nor as a description of the legalistic character of first-century Pharisaism, but as a theological interpretation by a Christian thinker of two ways of righteousness: legalism and faith. This is made clear in Romans 10, where Paul bemoans the fate of Israel in having failed to recognize Jesus as her Messiah and embrace the divine gift of a free salvation. Why was Israel blind to the claims of Christ? Paul's answer is that there are two ways of righteousness, and because Israel pursued one way, they missed the other. Israel followed the "law of righteousness" (Rom. 9:31, KJV), i.e., the law which revealed the will of God and showed what a right relationship with God was; but Israel failed to attain to that goal because they misused the law by making it a means of attaining righteousness by their own works instead of through faith (Rom. 9:32). Thus they showed themselves to be ignorant of the righteousness which comes from God and is received by faith; instead, they tried to establish their own righteousness of works and did not submit to the righteousness of God through faith (Rom. 10:1-3). In these words, Paul makes the fundamental issue clear: the establishing of one's own righteousness (by works), or submission to the righteousness of God (by faith).

In writing as he does about the law, Paul is writing distinctly from a Christian viewpoint. His experience of justification through faith in Christ and the subsequent conflict with the Judaizers led him to insights which he could not have held as a Jew, and to a fundamental reinterpretation of the role of the law in redemptive history which was not understood even by the prophets.

THE BACKGROUND OF PAUL'S THOUGHT ABOUT THE LAW

To understand Paul's thought, we must interpret it against the threefold background of the role of the law in Old Testament religion, in Judaism, and in his own experience. The heart of Old Testament religion cannot be characterized as legalism, nor was the law given as the means of achieving a right relationship with God by obedience. On the contrary, the context of the law was the covenant which preceded and underlay the law; and the covenant was initiated by the gracious act of God. Israel was constituted God's people not because of merit gained by obedience to the law, but because of God's free election.[1] Israel belongs to God because he has revealed himself by delivering his people out of Egypt. The law was given as the means of binding Israel to her God. Obedience to the law did not constitute Israel God's people; rather, it provided Israel with a standard for obedience by which the covenant relationship might be preserved. "Thus the object of the law is to settle the relationship of the covenant-nation and of the individual to the God of the covenant and to the members of the nation who belong to the same God."[2] The reward for obedience to the law was preservation of the positive relationship to Yahweh. This is the meaning of Leviticus 18:5, that the man who obeys the law shall live, i.e., enjoy the blessings of God.[3] However, life was not a reward earned by good works; it was itself God's gift. This is illustrated by Deuteronomy 30:15-20 where Moses lays before the people the choice of life or death, which is determined by whether or not Israel chooses the Word of God. "Only by faith, i.e., by cleaving to the God of salvation, will the righteous have life (cf. Hab. 2:4; Amos 5:4, 14; Jer. 38:20). It is obvious that life is here understood as a gift."[4] Furthermore, the obedience demanded by the law could not be satisfied by a mere legalism, for the law itself demanded love for God (Deut. 6:5; 10:12) and for neighbor (Lev. 19:18). Obedience to the law of God was an expression of trust in God; and only those who offered God such trust were really his people.

One of the most important factors in the old covenant was the twofold character of the people of God. On the one hand, they constituted a theocracy—a nation; but they were also a spiritual people. Membership in the nation required obedience to external commands, e.g., circumcision; but circumcision of the flesh did not make a man right with God; there must also be a circumcision of the heart (Jer. 4:4; Deut. 10:16). When the nation proved disobedient to the demands of the covenant, the prophets announced that God had rejected the nation as a whole and would raise up in her place a faithful remnant righteous in heart as well as in deed. Thus there is found even in the Old Testament the distinction between the nation and the "church," between physical Israel and the true, spiritual Israel,[5] who have the law written on their hearts (Jer. 31:33).

In the intertestamental period, a fundamental change occurred in the role of the law in the life of the people. The importance of the law overshadows the concept of the covenant and becomes the condition of membership in God's people. Even more importantly, observance of the law becomes the basis of God's verdict upon the individual. Resurrection will be the reward of those who have been devoted to the law (2 Macc. 7:9). The law is the basis of the hope of the faithful (Test. Jud. 26:1), of justification (Apoc. Bar. 51:3), of salvation (Apoc. Bar. 51:7), of righteousness (Apoc. Bar. 57:6), of life (IV Ez. 7:21; 9:31). Obedience to the law will even bring God's kingdom and transform the entire sin-cursed world (Jub. 23). Thus the law attains the position of an intermediary between God and man.

This new role of the law characterizes Rabbinic Judaism; and for this reason, the basic starting point of the Old Testament is characteristically and decisively altered and invalidated. The Torah becomes the one and only mediator between God and man; all other relationships between God and man, Israel, or the world are subordinated to the Torah. Both righteousness and life in the world to come are secured by obeying the law. "The more study of the law, the more life" . . . "If [a man] has gained for himself words of the law, he has gained for himself life in the world to come" (Pirke Aboth 2:7).[6]

This does not mean that the Judaism out of which Paul came was utterly destitute of any spiritual values. There were circles in Judaism where the higher elements of inner devotion and piety were coupled with strict obedience to the law.[7] Nor are we to forget that at the heart of first-century Jewish personal devotion as well as the synagogue worship was the recital of the Shema with its call to love God with the whole heart.[8] However, the tendency to externalism is evident even at this point, for the very repetition of the Shema was seen as a submitting to the reign of God.[9]

It is true that repentance played a large role in Jewish piety. While the Jews never despaired about the "fulfillability" of the law, it was nevertheless a real problem.[10] All of the commandments, both written and oral, must be kept. "To violate one of them was equivalent to rejecting the whole Law and refusing God's yoke" (*Sifre* on Num. 15:22).[11] However, salvation did not depend upon faultless conformity to the law. Man is indwelt by an evil impulse as well as a good impulse, and therefore no man can attain to sinless perfection.[12]

Therefore the "righteous" man is not he who obeys the law flawlessly, but he alone who *strives* to regulate his life by the law. The sincerity and supremacy of this purpose and the strenuous endeavor to accomplish it are the marks of a righteous man.[13] Because God knew that man could not perfectly keep the law because of the evil impulse which God himself had implanted in his creature, God provided repentance as the way by which man's sins could be forgiven. Repentance therefore must be coeval with the law, and is one of the seven things pre-existent before creation.[14] Repentance plays such a large role in Judaism that Moore calls it "the Jewish doctrine of salvation."[15] The righteous man, therefore, is not the man who actually succeeds in keeping the law, but the man who intends to, strives to do so, and is repentant when he fails. This repentance is the sole but inexorable condition of God's forgiveness, and is efficacious however great the sin may have been, or however late a man comes to repentance.[16] Repentance is purification of the inner man, and so annuls the sinner's past that he is in effect a new creation.[17] Sacrifices were carried out because the law commanded them; but Judaism had no theory of atonement. It was repentance that secured the efficacy of the sacrifices.[18]

It is this background in Jewish thought that leads Schoeps to say that whether a man actually fulfills the law or not, the mere intention to fulfill it brings a man close to God. This good intention is an "affirmation of the covenant, which precedes the law."[19] Paul, however, he says, was fatally ignorant of the Jewish doctrine of repentance. He failed to understand the relationship between the covenant and the law, and isolated the law from the controlling context of God's covenant with Israel.[20]

Schoeps bases his argument upon the Old Testament view of the relationship between covenant and law, attributing this understanding to Judaism. However, the reverse appears to be the historical fact: viz., that Judaism had in reality substituted the law for the covenant, or identified the covenant with the law. Schoeps in effect admits this when he says, "By covenant is meant nothing other than the Torah."[21] It is significant that the concept of the covenant plays a very small role in rabbinic writings[22] and tends to be identified with circumcision and the Sabbath.[23] Moore on the basis of Mishnah Sanhedrin 10.1 argues that eternal life is ultimately assured to every Israelite[24] "on the ground of the original election of the people by the free grace of God, prompted not by its merits, collective or individual, but solely by God's love."[25] This conclusion is difficult to sustain, if for no other reason than that of the exclusion of certain classes of Israelites from eternal life in the paragraphs that follow. It is refuted by the discussion of the fate of the righteous, the wicked, and the middle class whose righteousness and sins balanced each other. The righteous enter at once into eternal life. Certain extremely wicked classes of people will be locked up to punishment in hell forever. Others, less wicked, together with the wicked of the nations, are thrown into hell to be punished for twelve months and then destroyed.[26] As to the great majority of Israelites who were half righteous and half sinful, the schools of Hillel and Shammai differed. The School of Hillel maintained that God in mercy would incline the balance to the side of mercy and not send them into hell at all; the School of Shammai held that they would be plunged into hell but would come up healed.[27] While it is true that it was God's kindness which gave the law to Israel, thus providing a basis for salvation, salvation itself is dependent upon good works, including the good work of repentance. This conclusion is strongly supported by the numerous references in Jewish literature to the books in which the good works of the righteous are recorded,[28] treasuries in which good works are stored up,[29] scales on which the merits and demerits are weighed.[30] God's grace grants forgiveness to the repentant man who has transgressed the law, but the devout man who fulfills the law, insofar as he fulfills it, does not need grace.

In any case, it is clear that Paul's life as a Jew was one of legalistic obedience to the law. He himself tells us that he was a committed Jew, a Pharisee who was blameless in his obedience to the letter of the law (Phil. 3:5-6). He was outstanding in his zeal not only for the written law but also for the oral scribal traditions (Gal. 1:14).

In view of these clear statements, it is impossible to accept the autobiographical interpretation of Romans[31] which pictures Paul torn by an inward struggle which plunged his soul into darkness and confusion, making him feel that the law had broken him and hope was almost gone.[32] In fact, the key to Paul's understanding of the law lies in the fact that his very devotion to the law had led to pride (Phil. 3:4, 7) and boasting (Rom. 2:17, 23). Boasting is the antithesis of faith (Rom. 4:2) for it means the effort to establish a human righteousness of works (Rom. 3:27) which seeks glory before God and which relies on itself rather than on God. This human pride and boasting is an affront to the very character of God, who alone must receive glory and before whom no human being may boast (1 Cor. 1:29). The only object for man's boasting is God himself (1 Cor. 1:31; 2 Cor. 10:17).[33]

Here is the shocking fact that compelled Paul to a complete re-evaluation of the law. It was his very zeal for the law which had blinded him to the revelation of God's righteousness in Christ. What he as a Jew had thought was righteousness, he now realizes to be the very essence of sin, for his pride in his own righteousness (Phil. 3:9) had blinded him to the revelation of the divine righteousness in Christ. Only the divine intervention on the Damascus road shattered his pride and self-righteousness and brought him to a humble acceptance of the righteousness of God.

THE LAW IN THE MESSIANIC AGE

Many features of Paul's interpretation of the law not only find no parallel in Judaism, but in fact so differ from Jewish thought that modern Jewish scholars refuse to accept his claim to have been a Palestinian rabbi but insist that he represents a distorted Judaism of the Diaspora.[34] On the contrary, Paul represents a fresh Christian interpretation which can be understood only from Paul's eschatological perspective. With Christ, the messianic age has been inaugurated. In Christ, "the old has passed away, behold, the new has come" (2 Cor. 5:17). Before he was in Christ, Paul understood the law κατὰ σάρκα, from a human point of view, in terms of the standards of the old aeon, even as he interpreted all his experience (2 Cor. 5:16). Viewed κατὰ σάρκα, the law was the basis of good works, which led to pride and boasting. Viewed κατὰ πνεῦμα, from the perspective of the new age in Christ, the law assumes an entirely different role in God's redemptive purpose. The prophets had foretold a day when God would make a new covenant with his people, when the law would be no longer primarily an outward written code but a law implanted within men, written on their hearts (Jer. 31:33). This promise of a new dimension of inwardness does not carry with it the complete abolition of the Mosaic law. On the basis of such Old Testament promises, the Jews debated the role the law would play in the messianic age and in the world to come. Moore concludes that in the messianic age, the law would be more faithfully studied and better applied than in this world; and in the age to come, although much of the law would be no longer applicable because of the changed conditions on the new earth, the law would continue to express the will of God, but God himself would be the teacher.[35]

With Christ a new era has come in which the law plays a new and different role. Paul designates these two eras of the law and the gospel as two covenants. The old covenant is one of the "letter" ($\gamma\rho\acute{\alpha}\mu\mu\alpha$), and is a dispensation ($\delta\iota\alpha\kappa\sigma\nu\acute{\iota}\alpha$) of condemnation and death, while the new covenant is one of the Spirit, a dispensation of life and righteousness (2 Cor. 3:6–18). These words do not refer to two ways of interpreting Scripture: a literal and a spiritual or allegorical approach. They contrast the ages of the law and of Christ as two different roles of the law. Under the old covenant, the law was an external written code which set before men the will of God. When they failed, it condemned them to death. The new covenant in this passage says nothing explicitly about the permanence of the law. The difference in the new age is that the Holy Spirit has been given to men to write the law upon their hearts, as Jeremiah foretold, and thus the law is no longer merely an external written code but an inward life-giving power which produces righteousness.[36]

Most interpreters of this passage have overlooked the fact that since the Holy Spirit is an eschatological gift, the entire passage has an eschatological orientation. The new age, which is the age of Christ and the Spirit, has come in fulfillment of Jeremiah 31,[37] even while the old age goes on.

While this passage in Second Corinthians says nothing about the permanence of the law, Paul tells the Romans, $\tau\acute{\epsilon}\lambda\sigma\varsigma$ $\gamma\grave{\alpha}\rho$ $\nu\acute{\sigma}\mu\sigma\nu$ $\chi\rho\iota\sigma\tau\grave{\sigma}\varsigma$ $\epsilon\grave{\iota}\varsigma$ $\delta\iota\kappa\alpha\iota\sigma\sigma\acute{\nu}\nu\eta\nu$ $\pi\alpha\nu\tau\grave{\iota}$ $\tau\hat{\omega}$ $\pi\iota\sigma\tau\epsilon\acute{\nu}\sigma\nu\tau\iota$ (For Christ is [the] end of [the] law unto righteousness to everyone who believes, Rom. 10:4). This verse can be rendered in two different ways. "Christ is the end of the law with the objective of righteousness for everyone who believes." That is, Christ has brought the law to its end in order that a righteousness based on faith alone may be available to all men. Another rendering is, "Christ is the end of the law so far as righteousness is concerned for everyone who believes." That is, the law is not itself abolished, but it has come to its end as a way of righteousness, for in Christ, righteousness is by faith, not by works.

In view of the fact that Paul has just contrasted the righteousness of God with that of the law, and continues immediately with the righteousness of the law (vs. 5), the latter rendering is preferable.[38] Paul does not affirm the total abrogation of the law in order that by its abrogation righteousness might come to believers.[39] He affirms the end of the law in its connection with righteousness. God has now revealed a righteousness in Christ apart from the law, with the result that law as a way of righteousness has come to an end for the believer. This is not true historically; the Jews continue to practice the law. It is true *heilsgeschichtlich*—for men of faith.

This is true because Christ is the end of the law. Τέλος can mean both end and goal, and both meanings are to be seen here. Christ has brought the era of the law to its end because he has fulfilled all that the law demands.

Paul expounds the life of the believer in the new age in several different ways. The new age is the age of life; and since the believer has been identified with Christ in his death and resurrection, he is dead to the old life, including the rule of the law. Paul uses the metaphor of a woman being freed from her husband when he dies, and applies it by saying that it is the believer who has died with Christ who is therefore free from the law (Rom. 7:4). Therefore we no longer serve God under bondage to a written external code but with the new life of the Spirit (Rom. 7:6). It was the law itself, which had become a basis of boasting, and therefore of sin, which convinced Paul that he must die to the reign of law (Gal. 2:19).

An apparent contradiction appears in Paul's thought when he insists that the believer is no longer under law, but at the same time, according to the Acts, approves of the law for Jewish Christians (Acts 21:20-26), and even circumcised Timothy when he joined Paul in missionary work because he was half Jewish (Acts 16:3). However, this contradiction corresponds to Paul's eschatological perspective. While believers have experienced the freedom of the new age in Christ, they still live in the present evil age. The law with its ceremonial demands belongs to this world—the old order. The proper attitude for men of the new age toward the old age is not a negative one but one of transcendence: "For neither circumcision counts for anything, nor uncircumcision, but a new creature," because circumcision belongs to the world, and the man in Christ has been crucified to the world (Gal. 6:14-15).

An application of this principle is that Paul himself as a Jew observed the law when he was in a Jewish environment (1 Cor. 9:20). As a man in Christ, he was no longer under law, and therefore, where the human situation required it for his ministry to the Gentiles, he "became as one outside the law" (1 Cor. 9:21). This involves, admittedly, a seeming inconsistency in conduct; but the very inconsistency rests upon the consistent application of a profound theological truth: that Christians belong to two worlds at once and have obligations to both orders.[40]

THE LAW AS THE WILL OF GOD

Paul never conceived of the claims of the law coming to their end because of any imperfection in the law itself. The law is and remains the law of God (Rom. 7:22, 25). The law is not sinful (Rom. 7:7) but is "holy and just and good" (Rom. 7:12) because it comes from God ("spiritual," Rom. 7:14).

At this point, it is important to note that Paul can speak of the law from several different points of view. The Greek word νόμος is not the equivalent of the Hebrew *torah*. Νόμος is fundamentally "custom," hardening into what we call "law," and is human in its perspective. *Torah* means "instruction" and is used not only of the legislation which God gave to be obeyed but also of divine instructions and teachings. In its broadest sense, it designates the divine revelation as a whole.[41] Under the influence of the Old Testament, Paul uses νόμος to designate not only legislation—"the law of commandments and ordinances" (Eph. 2:15)—but also, like *torah*, to refer to the Old Testament, where no legislation is involved.[42] In still other places, Paul uses νόμος in a Greek way to designate a principle (Rom. 3:27; 7:23, 25; 8:2).[43]

Thus we can understand how Paul can reflect the Jewish point of view that the law is a standard for life by which he as a Pharisee lived blamelessly (Phil. 3:6). This level of interpretation had led him to pride in his own righteous achievements and to boasting. At the same time, there is a deeper demand of the law, for the law expresses the total will of God. The law itself witnesses to the righteousness of God (Rom. 3:21). The law's demand is such that only love can satisfy it (Rom. 13:8).

When Paul says that the mind set on the flesh "is hostile to God; it does not submit to God's law, indeed it cannot" (Rom. 8:7), he is referring to more than legal statutes. Hostility to God is in reality rejection of the law of God; what God's law requires is not merely outward obedience but an obedient and submissive heart. Israel's problem lay precisely at this point. Pursuing a "law of righteousness," i.e., a law which would make men right with God, they failed to attain this very righteousness because they refused to submit to God's righteousness by faith but instead sought a righteousness by works which is no true righteousness at all (Rom. 9:31-32; 10:1-2). The human righteousness which is achieved by works (Phil. 3:6) is itself a denial of true righteousness; it is "a righteousness of my own" (Phil. 3:9), and is therefore a ground of boasting (Rom. 2:23; Eph. 2:9); and this very boasting is the essence of sin, for it is the exaltation of self against God. Boasting in one's own righteousness is equivalent to having confidence in the flesh (Phil. 3:3). Legal righteousness leads to this selfish, sinful pride and frustrates the true righteousness demanded by God. When the Jews boast in the law and sit in prideful judgment on those who do not have the law, they show by this very fact that they do not know true righteousness (Rom. 2:17-21). The very act of judging convicts them of being sinners (Rom. 2:1). Sin is man's ambition to put himself in the place of God and so be his own lord. This is precisely what the judge does when he assumes the right to sit in judgment on his fellow creatures.[44] When Paul accuses the Jews of inconsistency for breaking the law at the very points where they condemn others—stealing, adultery, temple robbing—he must have had the higher demand of the law for an inner righteousness in mind, for instances of such flagrant conduct did not characterize first-century Jews, who were in fact recognized by the Gentiles for their high moral standards. Paul must be referring to robbing God of the honor due him, spiritual adultery, and of profaning the devotion due God alone by exalting themselves as judge and lord over their fellow creatures (Rom. 2:17-24).[45] Paul immediately goes on to say that circumcision—the symbol of all law-keeping —is really of the heart and not of the flesh, and to be a true Jew is to have a right heart toward God (Rom. 2:25-29).

If then the law in fact embodies the full will of God, it follows ideally that full conformity to the law would lead to life (Rom. 7:10). Those who do the law will be justified (Rom. 2:13). But at this point, Paul goes beyond Judaism. Judaism based salvation upon conformity to the law, but recognized that most men did not perfectly keep the law. Therefore, it had to mix its doctrine of salvation by obedience to the law with a doctrine of forgiveness and repentance, by which God in his mercy grants salvation to men who are partly righteous and partly sinners.[46]

Paul sees that this involved two contradictory principles: works and grace. He therefore insists upon something that no Jewish rabbi would accept,[47] viz., that if righteousness is obedience to law, then obedience must be perfect—without a single flaw. One who submits to the law must keep the *whole* law (Gal. 5:3). Any man who does not do *all things* written in the law is cursed (Gal. 3:10). Paul would assent to the words of James that whoever obeys the entire law but fails in a single point is guilty of being a lawbreaker and stands under condemnation (Jas. 2:10).

The problem of perfect fulfillment of the law is most acute at the point where the law demands more than conformity to outward regulations. This is revealed when Paul says that a man may accept circumcision and yet not keep the law (Rom. 2:25). On the surface, this is a nonsensical statement, for the very act of circumcision is obedience to the law. When Paul goes on to say that true circumcision is a matter of the heart and not something external and physical (Rom. 2:28-29), it is clear that obedience to the law "does not mean carrying out the detailed precepts written in the Pentateuch, but fulfilling that relation with God to which the law points; and this proves in the last resort to be a relation not of legal obedience but of faith."[48]

THE FAILURE OF THE LAW

Although the law remains for Paul the righteous and holy expression of the will of God, the law has failed to make men righteous before God. It is impossible for a man to be justified by the works of the law (Gal. 2:16). In fact, there is no possible law that can make a man right with God (Gal. 3:21). The reason for this failure is twofold.

The most fundamental reason is that the weakness and the sinfulness of man render him incapable of giving the obedience the law demands. The condition of the human heart is such that no law could help it. The weakness of the flesh (Rom. 8:3) and the sinfulness of human nature (Rom. 7:23) could not be changed by the law. The idea of some rabbis that man's evil impulses could be overcome by study of the law,[49] Paul would firmly reject.

The reason why the law cannot make sinful men righteous is that it is an external code, whereas the sinful hearts of men need a transforming inward power. The law is a written code, not a life imparted by God's Spirit (Rom. 7:6). This idea is extended in the contrast between the new and the old covenant. The old covenant of law consisted of commands written on tables of stone, which could only declare the will of God but could not provide to sinful men the power to obey God's will. Therefore, even though it was glorious, the written code condemns men as sinners and places them under the judgment of death. "The written code kills," whereas what men need is life (2 Cor. 3:6).

THE REINTERPRETATION OF THE LAW

In reflecting upon the failure of the law in contrast with the work of Christ to bring him to a knowledge of the righteousness of God, Paul achieves a new interpretation of the role of the law in God's overall redemptive purposes. First, he explains the inability of the law to procure salvation by showing that this was not the divine intention. The law is secondary to the promise, and God's way of salvation by faith is found in the promise.

To the Galatians, Paul argues that God made a covenant of promise with Abraham long before he gave the law to Moses (Gal. 3:15–18). Making a play on the word διαθήκη, which can mean both will-testament and covenant, Paul points out that as a valid human testament cannot be contested or altered by additions, so the promise of God given to Abraham cannot be invalidated by the law which came later.[50] And since this covenant with Abraham was one of promise, the possibility of righteousness by works is excluded, for promise and law are mutually exclusive. The promise is no longer promise if it is conditioned by the law.[51]

This idea is further supported in Romans by the argument that Abraham did not have the law but was accounted righteous by faith (Rom. 4:1-5). Paul points out that this righteousness was attained by faith even before the sign of circumcision had been given. Circumcision, then, in its true significance does not belong to the law but is a sign and seal of justifying faith (Rom. 4:9-12).

It is disappointing to the modern student of Paul and Judaism that Paul does not work out a consistent pattern of the relationship between covenant and law. Thus he uses διαθήκη of the covenant of promise made with Abraham (Gal. 3), but he also uses it of the covenant of the law (2 Cor. 3:14), as well as of the covenant in Christ. Quite certainly, while Paul says that the law was a dispensation of death, he would not maintain that the old covenant of the law meant death to all who were under that covenant. On the contrary, the implication of the line of thought in Galatians 3 and Romans 4 is that all Israelites who trusted God's covenant of promise to Abraham and did not use the law as a way of salvation by works were assured of salvation. This becomes explicit in the case of David who, though under the law, pronounced a blessing on the man to whom God reckons righteousness apart from works (Rom. 4:6–7). When Paul speaks of the *coming* of faith (Gal. 3:25), he does not mean that previously no one had ever exercised saving faith. On the contrary, for Paul, faith appeared with Abraham; but faith could be frustrated when the law was made a basis of human righteousness and boasting.

If salvation is by way of promise and not law, what was the role of the law in God's redemptive purpose? In answering this question, Paul comes to conclusions which were both novel and quite unacceptable to Judaism.[52] The law was added ($\pi\alpha\rho\epsilon\iota\sigma\hat{\eta}\lambda\theta\epsilon\nu$) not to save men from their sins but to define sin (Rom. 3:20; 5:13; 5:20; Gal. 3:19). By declaring the will of God, by showing what God forbids, the law shows what sin is. By forbidding coveting, it shows that coveting is sin (Rom. 7:7). Thus the power of sin is the law (1 Cor. 15:56), for only by the law is sin clearly defined. Sayings about the law making sin to increase (Rom. 5:20) do not mean that it was the law which actually brought sin into being and made man more sinful than he was without the law. The law is not itself sinful or sin-producing (Rom. 7:7). Rather, the law discloses man's true situation, that his accountability to God as a sinner may be revealed (Rom. 3:19).

Thus the law is an instrument of condemnation (Rom. 5:13), wrath (Rom. 4:15), and death (Rom. 7:9; 2 Cor. 3:6). It is not the law itself which produces this tragic situation; it is sin in man which makes the law an instrument of death (Rom. 7:13). The dispensation of the law can be called a dispensation of death (2 Cor. 3:7), of slavery to the world (Gal. 4:1-10), a covenant of slavery (Gal. 4:21-31), a period of childhood when one is under the control of guardians (Gal. 3:23-26).[53]

Certainly Paul does not mean to suggest that all men who lived between Moses and Christ were in such bondage to sin and death that there was no salvation until Christ came. His reference to David (Rom. 4:6-8) disproves that. The promise antedates the law and was valid both before and after its fulfillment in Christ. Nor does Paul mean that this was his experience as a Jew under the law. This is his understanding of what the law, apart from the promise, really accomplishes. Paul's argument in both Romans and Galatians is not designed to instruct Jews how they should understand the law, but to keep Gentile Christians, who had no racial tie to the law as Jewish Christians did, from exchanging salvation by grace for salvation by the works of the law.[54]

It is from this same Christian perspective that the much contested passage in Romans 7:13-25 is to be interpreted. The older autobiographical interpretation is very difficult in light of Paul's own descriptions of his Jewish life in Galatians 1:14 and Philippians 3:5-6.[55] It is equally difficult to understand the passage to describe the experience of the defeated Christian who still relies on the flesh in contrast to the victorious Christian who has learned to rely on the Spirit (Rom. 8).[56] Paul's concern in this passage is not life in the flesh but the nature of the law. Is the law sin? (Rom. 7:7). No; but because sin dwells in man, the holy law shows sin to be sin and thus becomes an instrument of death. But it is sin, not the law, which brings death (Rom. 7:10-11).

This theme is further expanded in verses 13-24. The entire chapter embodies a Christian understanding of the actual plight of man under the law, whether this corresponds to his conscious experience or not. As a Pharisee, Saul was quite satisfied with his obedience to the law and found therein a cause for pride and boasting. But as a Christian, Paul understands that he was deceived because he had misused the law. Only in the light of his life in Christ can he understand what his situation under the law really was; and only as a Christian can he understand why the law can in fact only condemn a man to death when it is itself holy and just and good. The reason is not the sinful nature of the law but the sinful nature of man. Thus Romans 7 is a picture of existence under the law understood from a Christian perspective.[57] The will of God, therefore, is a delight to man, and he desires to fulfill the highest demand of the law to love both God and neighbor. As Paul looks back on his life as a Jew under the law, he realizes, contrary to his previous conviction, that he had not fulfilled the law. Because of sin residing in his flesh, he was incapable of providing the righteousness God requires, for the good demanded by the law is not mere outward formal obedience, but the demand of God for true righteousness.[58] Of this, man is incapable—so incapable, in fact, it is as though his own will is overcome completely by sin which rules his life (vss. 17, 20). Freedom from this bondage to sin and death is found only in Jesus Christ.

THE PERMANENCE OF THE LAW

By fulfilling the promise given to Abraham, Christ has brought to an end the age of the law and inaugurated the age of Christ, which means freedom from bondage and the end of the law for the believer. However, it is clear that inasmuch as Paul always regards the law as holy and just and good, he never thinks of the law as being totally abolished. It remains the expression of the will of God.

This is evident from his frequent assertion that redemption in Christ enables believers in some real sense to fulfill the law. In Christ, God has done what the law could not do—viz., condemned sin in the flesh, that the just requirement of the law might be fulfilled in those who walk by the Spirit (Rom. 8:3-4). Here is paradox: by being freed from the law, we uphold the law (Rom. 3:31). It is obvious that the new life in Christ enables the Christian to keep the law not as an external code but in terms of its higher demand—i.e., at the very point where the law was powerless because it was an external written code. Thus, Paul repeats that the essential Christian ethic of love, which is a gift of the Holy Spirit (1 Cor. 13; Gal. 5:22), is the fulfilling of the law. The whole law is fulfilled in one word, "You shall love your neighbor as yourself" (Gal. 5:14). In place of the law as a written code is now the law of Christ. This "new law" cannot be reduced to specific rules but goes far beyond legislation. No set of rules can tell one how to bear the burdens of another (Gal. 6:2); only love can dictate such conduct. However, the law of Christ, which is the law of love, does fulfill the law. Love will not commit adultery or lie or steal or covet, or do any wrong to one's neighbor (Rom. 13:8-10).

Probably Paul refers to this same law of Christ when he expounds his own personal relationship to law. As a man in Christ, he is no longer under the law, and therefore he can minister to Gentiles as though he were a Gentile who had no law (ἄνομος). Yet he is not therefore an antinomian (ἄνομος θεοῦ) but ἔννομος χριστοῦ—"subject to the law of Christ."[59] Because he is motivated by love, he adapts himself to men of all kinds of conditions to bring them the gospel.[60]

The permanence of the law is reflected further in the fact that Paul appeals to specific commands in the law as the norm for

Christian conduct. He appeals to several specific commandments (ἐντολαί) of the Decalogue which are fulfilled by love (Rom. 13:8–10). His reference to "any other commandment" designates everything in the law which relates to one's neighbor. Yet it was the character of the law as ἐντολαί which marked its externality. Again, Paul quotes the command to love father and mother as the first commandment with a promise (Eph. 6:2). It is clear that the law continues to be the expression of the will of God for conduct, even for those who are no longer under the law.

It is quite clear, however, that the permanent aspect of the law is the ethical and not the ceremonial. "For neither circumcision counts for anything nor uncircumcision, but keeping the commandments of God" (1 Cor. 7:19). Most of the studies on Paul emphasize the fact that Paul does not explicitly distinguish between the ethical and ceremonial aspects of the law. This is of course true; but the implicit distinction is unavoidable and should be stressed. Although circumcision is a command of God and a part of the law, Paul sets circumcision in contrast to the commandments, and in so doing separates the ethical from the ceremonial—the permanent from the temporal. Thus he can commend the ἐντολαί θεοῦ to Gentiles, and yet adamantly reject the ceremonial ἐντολαί, such as circumcision, foods, feasts, and even Sabbath keeping (Col. 2:16), for these are but a shadow of the reality which has come in Christ.

Thus Christ has brought the law as a way of righteousness and as a ceremonial code to its end, but the law as the expression of the will of God is permanent; and the man indwelt by the Holy Spirit and thus energized by love is enabled to fulfill the law as men under the law never could.

V

WORD AND POWER
(1 Corinthians 1:17—2:5)

William Childs Robinson, Jr.

Paul's treatise on the word of the cross is within the topic, the power of God, a topic which is present here neither as an abstract concept nor merely in an assertion of ontological contrast between divine omnipotence and mortal frailty. There is contrast, and it provides the background for the treatise, but the emphasis, instead of being on the ontological, is upon the actual, expressed in the familiar biblical mockery of human presumption before God:

> For it is written,
> "I will destroy the wisdom of the wise,
>   and the cleverness of the clever I will thwart."
> Where is the wise man? Where is the scribe? Where is the debater of this age? Has not God made foolish the wisdom of the world?" (1 Corinthians 1:19-20).

Such biblical contrasts were intended, by ridiculing an inappropriate understanding of the actual human situation before God, to restore a right understanding of man in his relation to God, a wisdom having its origin in the fear of the Lord. That this was also Paul's intention is evident from the sharp contrasts beginning with reference to the Corinthians' lowly station in life (1 Cor. 1:26-28) which Paul directed toward the conclusion

> that no human being might boast in the presence of God. . . . therefore, as it is written, "Let him who boasts, boast of the Lord" (1 Cor. 1:29, 31).

Paul's intention is also evident from the line of thought immediately following the mockery:

> For since, in the wisdom of God, the world did not know
> God through wisdom, it pleased God through the folly of
> what we preach to save those who believe (1 Cor. 1:21).

Here, too, the aim is not a theoretical knowledge of God but an acknowledgment of God which implies a relationship to God. If, as seems likely, the reference to "the wisdom of God" is a reference to God's creation,[1] the thought is essentially the same as that in Romans 1:19-21, where "what can be known about God"—"his eternal power and deity"—is "plain" to man, "perceived" and "known" by man, and yet without man's giving of "glory" and "thanks," whereby actual acknowledgment does not accompany the perception that God does exist in his eternal power and deity.

Against this background Paul's thesis is that the word of the cross is the power of God, the means whereby God was "pleased . . . to save those who believe" (1 Cor. 1:18, 21), with which Romans 1 again provides a parallel: "I am not ashamed of the gospel: it is the power of God for salvation to every one who has faith . . ." (Romans 1:16). These references to the power of God are Paul's formulation of the widespread conviction that man is capable of knowing God only if God enables him.

The concrete reference of the word of the cross is evident further in that the treatise is in place and integrally so, for not only has the integrity of 1 Corinthians 1-4 gone unchallenged even in the literary analyses of Johannes Weiss and his followers,[2] but it also is clear that the treatise is organically part of Paul's response to the disturbing news Chloe's people brought, that there was dissension in the Corinthian church (1 Cor. 1:11).[3] The passage is therefore, precisely in its focus upon the word of the cross, concretely applied theology.

I

Paul introduced the treatise on the word of the cross with the statement, "For Christ did not send me to baptize but to preach the gospel, and not with eloquent wisdom, lest the cross of Christ be emptied of its power" (1 Cor. 1:17). He concluded the section by referring to his initial preaching in Corinth (1 Cor. 2:

1-5). To understand these statements we must try to discover how Paul related the references to his past ministry and the crisis current in Corinth.

While a question as to the content of the word of the cross would be oversimplified by an alternative such as the fact of Jesus' death (and its manner—by crucifixion) *or* the theological implications of the crucifixion in Paul's understanding of the existence of the Christian believer, there are prominent instances in current interpretation of the passage which—although their authors would presumably reject the above as a false alternative—put the emphasis well over toward the fact and manner side of such a scale. There is no question that Paul put major soteriological significance on the death of Christ; the question posed here is that of the locus of emphasis in this passage.

At the outset (1:17) two things seem foremost: safeguarding the content of the cross and, to that end, preaching the gospel. Initially the preaching is described only negatively: not with eloquent wisdom. When Paul says "lest the cross of Christ be emptied" (1:17), are we to infer that the Corinthians had rejected some content belonging to the fact of Jesus' death or, more precisely, belonging to the mode of death, crucifixion? Such impressions are fostered by the graphic quality of the New English Bible translation at several points.[4]

> 1 Cor 1:23: We proclaim Christ—yes, Christ nailed to the cross . . .
> 1 Cor. 2:2: Jesus Christ—Christ nailed to the cross.
> 1 Cor. 1:17: so that the fact of Christ on his cross might have its full weight.

With these compare the translation at

> Gal. 3:1: You stupid Galatians! . . . before whose eyes Jesus Christ was openly displayed upon his cross!

Although Paul knew both the fact and the manner of Jesus' death, his writings give no evidence that he was concerned either to prove it or to portray it. He quoted a traditional formulation containing an assertion of the facticity of that death: "he was buried" (1 Cor. 15:4), but at that point his topic required no exposition of this part of the formula. Furthermore, it is evident that some early Christians were interested in portraying the death of Christ (though not with modern historiography's desire to portray it *wie es eigentlich gewesen ist*), the Passion tradition in Mark presenting it in scriptural terms and the Lucan account showing Jesus dying as a faithful martyr. But despite his knowledge of the fact and the manner of Jesus' death, Paul's use of the words "cross" and "crucify" does not seem to have been controlled by a wish to specify the manner of Jesus' death.

Chrysostom took Galatians 3:1 to mean a graphic description of the manner of Jesus' death, a view which has repeatedly found adherents, although it rests on inadequate grounds.[5] In the term "Christ crucified" (Gal. 3:1; 1 Cor. 1:23; 2:2) Paul used a perfect participle, which in Greek usually expressed a presently existing consequence of a past occurrence. As E. DeW. Burton put it,

> To express the idea "in the act of being crucified" would require a present participle, if the thought were "in the act of being affixed to the cross," and probably if it were "hanging on the cross."[6]

Directed toward delineation of the past event, the emphatically graphic NEB translation obscures what Paul actually did say with this participle: though Christ did not remain dead, but is alive, he remains—as the risen Christ—the crucified one.

The impression that the Corinthians had rejected some content belonging to the manner of Jesus' death is also fostered by a widespread interpretation of *skandalon* at 1 Corinthians 1:23, to which the NEB translation also gives support:

> For Jews demand signs and Greeks seek wisdom, but we preach Christ crucified, a stumbling block to Jews and folly to Gentiles ... (RSV)

Compare the New English Bible:

> Jews call for miracles, Greeks look for wisdom; but we proclaim Christ—yes, Christ nailed to the cross; and though this is a stumbling-block to Jews and folly to Greeks, yet ...

The *skandalon* of Paul's preaching Christ crucified has often been interpreted from the manner of death: Jews would have included crucifixion under the curse of Deuteronomy 21:23 and so would have stumbled at Messianic claims for one who had been crucified,[7] and Gentiles would have scorned claims to majesty for such a one, though without recourse to the Bible. Add to this that Paul himself cited Deuteronomy 21:23 to proof-text the statement "Christ redeemed us from the curse of the law, having become a curse for us" (Gal. 3:13), and this explanation of the "stumbling block" of 1 Corinthians 1:23 may seem secured. I think it is not, and we return to this question later.

According to Walter Schmithals and Ulrich Wilckens, the trouble arose from denial of certain articles of the faith.[8] They think the Corinthians held a docetic (Gnostic) christology, where theological importance was put so exclusively upon the risen Christ that the earthly Jesus was held to be of no theological significance whatever—so that some of the Corinthian Christians anathematized the earthly Jesus (1 Cor. 12:3). Both Schmithals and Wilckens maintain, though in different ways, that "in Corinth a wisdom doctrine had replaced the cross,"[9] and that the Corinthian Christians, consistent with their christology, had denied any soteriological significance to the fact of Jesus' death. But this is untenable in view of the rhetorical question at 1 Corinthians 1:13 ("Paul wasn't crucified for you, was he?") and the traditional formula quoted in 1 Corinthians 15:3 ("Christ died for our sins . . ."), for a rhetorical question derives its force from the agreement to which it refers, and at 1 Corinthians 15 Paul would hardly have sabotaged his whole argument by beginning it with a statement his opponents would ridicule.

Wilckens went on to define the Corinthian position more exactly. They had rejected the saving significance of the cross because of their christology, which was not just generally Gnostic but precisely articulated, wherein "Wisdom" was a christological title of the exalted Christ. The weakness of this position is that it lacks support in the text. At 1 Corinthians 1:24, 30, Paul does refer to Christ as the "wisdom of God." In neither instance, however, is it evident that the apposition of "wisdom" is to be understood as equating Christ with a personified "Wisdom." The

christological equation which Wilckens claims, since he did not
establish it within 1 Corinthians 1:17—2:5, must rest on an equation of "the Lord of glory" (1 Cor. 2:8) with the "wisdom of God"
(2:6-7). Wilckens does not argue here from the meaning of
Paul's text, which asserts no such equation,[10] but derives his
opinion outside the text from the history-of-religions assumptions
with which he approaches the text. These assumptions have been
effectively challenged.[11]

The positions discussed thus far have not clarified the relation
of Paul's former mission to the present problem in Corinth. Paul
does not focus on the mere fact of Jesus' death or on its manner
as offensive, nor upon a Corinthian rejection of its soteriological
significance. Rather he puts the emphasis on the *preaching* of
Christ crucified ("the word of the cross" 1:18; "the folly of what
we preach" 1:21; "we preach Christ crucified" 1:23; "to know
nothing among you except Jesus Christ and him crucified" [NOT:
"I would think of nothing . . . ," NEB] 2:2; "my speech and my
message" 2:4).

To be sure Paul did preach Christ crucified, but his emphasis
here is neither on assertion of the fact nor on portrayal of the
manner of that death, but upon preaching the Christ who, though
dead, is risen and who, though risen, remains the crucified Christ.
Here Paul stresses the implications of that preaching for Christian
existence. And herein lay the link between his founding mission
and the current crisis, for he rejects the Corinthian assumption
that the mature Christian has been glorified out of an existence
determined by the word of the cross. The basis for their continued
existence as Christians is the same as the basis of their conversion.

II

To clarify further what Paul said of his preaching and especially
to see how he related his former preaching to the current crisis,
we need to know what he meant by saying his preaching was not
"with eloquent wisdom" and to clarify the meaning of *skandalon*
(and folly) at 1:23.

He introduced the discussion of the word of the cross by saying,
"Christ did not send me to baptize but to preach the gospel,

and not with eloquent wisdom, lest the cross of Christ be emptied."
There is a similar connection of terms at the conclusion of the
section on the word of the cross (2:1-5):

> When I came to you, brethren, I did not come proclaiming
> to you the testimony of God in lofty words or wisdom. For
> I decided to know nothing among you except Jesus Christ
> and him crucified. And I was with you in weakness and in
> much fear and trembling; and my speech and my message
> were not in plausible words of wisdom, but in demonstration
> of the Spirit and power, that your faith might not rest in the
> wisdom of men but in the power of God.

Here again preaching "in lofty words or wisdom" / "in plausible
words of wisdom" (2:1, 4) is rejected. But here that rejection is
followed not by the negative statement—"lest the cross of Christ
be emptied"—but is contrasted with the positive assertion that
Paul's preaching was marked by a "demonstration of the Spirit
and power" (2:4). This then confirms the meaning of "emptying"
the cross at 1:17 which Paul's usage elsewhere suggests, "to
render of no effect, to nullify." The RSV translates aptly: "lest
the cross of Christ be emptied of its power"—i.e., power from
God (see also 1:18, 24 ff.). Apparently Paul thought that to
preach "with eloquent wisdom" (1:17), "in lofty words or wisdom" (2:1), or in "plausible words of wisdom" (2:4) would not
be a "demonstration of the Spirit and power."

Thus Paul was not simply rejecting rhetorical skill,[12] whatever
may have been his own abilities as a public speaker (which we
will consider in this connection later). Nor did Paul oppose the
use of reason,[13] as if the content of the cross were its irrationality
and faith therefore a *credere quia absurdum*. Because he thought
it was his task in preaching to provide a "demonstration" of the
power of God, Paul rejected wisdom, for he saw it put in the
place of the divine power. This is clear from his use of *skandalon*.

There is, in addition to 1 Corinthians 1:23, one other Pauline
statement on the offense of the cross, Galatians 5:11: "But if I,
brethren, still preach circumcision, why am I still persecuted? In
that case the stumbling block of the cross has been removed." If
Paul were to preach the law as the way of salvation, the offense

of the cross would be removed. To maintain the offense of the cross, Paul in his preaching advocated neither wisdom nor the law. Not that he considered either to be intrinsically evil; both were gifts from God. In that sense Paul advocated both (see 1 Cor. 2:6-13; Rom. 7:7, 12), and the previous statement requires modification: Paul advocated neither law nor wisdom *as the way of salvation.* What is meant by those negatives is suggested by the phrase "wisdom of men" (1 Cor. 2:5) or "of this age" (2:6) and by the explicit statements at Romans 10:3:

> For, being ignorant of the righteousness that comes from God, and seeking to establish their own, they did not submit to God's righteousness.

His meaning has already become apparent from comparing 1 Corinthians 1:17 and 2:1-5 and is indeed the substance of the entire section on the word of the cross: the opposition of human wisdom and divine power. As Christ is the end of the law, so in Christ God has made foolish the wisdom of the world.

Paul may have known that the manner of Jesus' death was offensive to Jews and that among Gentiles such a death mocked claims to divine majesty. But he put the accents elsewhere. The word of the cross was a stumbling block in that it denied man's boast, his sinful self-reliance before God.

III

In Paul's view the problem in Corinth lay in a misunderstanding of the mode of possessing God's gifts.[14] He acknowledged that they had been richly blessed by God; it was more than conventional epistolary form which moved him to address the Corinthians (and the Galatians) as Christians. Despite the disagreement he considered them Christians, and in the opening of 1 Corinthians he acknowledged that

> the grace of God . . . was given you in Christ Jesus, that in every way you were enriched in him with all speech and all knowledge . . . so that you are not lacking in any spiritual gift . . . (1 Cor. 1:4-7).

Paul referred to his initial preaching of Christ crucified (and to their station in life, 1:26-31), in making the point that their present understanding of the Christian life denied the implications of their initial faith. From Paul's criticism at 3:1-4 it would seem they thought they had advanced to spiritual maturity, and his sarcasm at 4:7-8 implies their claim to have entered into full and final possession of God's eschatological blessings. For Paul their boast is the implicit denial of the power of God in the word of the cross.

The reference to his founding mission served a function other than just to remind them of their initial commitment, for without such a reminder Paul could still have expounded the implications of Christian faith. He referred to his initial ministry among them as a "demonstration of the Spirit and power" (1 Cor. 2:4). At issue, here and throughout his controversy with Corinth, was the demonstration of the presence of God's power. Members of the Corinthian church later demanded that Paul exhibit the proof that Christ was speaking in him (2 Cor. 13:3; cf. all of 2 Cor. 10-13); and here (1 Cor. 1-4) they are so sure of their full possession of God's power that they withdraw from fellowship and concern for others whom they presumably consider not to possess the power so fully as they do (1 Cor. 3:1-4; 4:6-8; 8:1; cf. Gal. 6:1-5).

Paul claimed that his initial mission exhibited the Spirit and power. How? Not by speaking in tongues,[15] for while the generalization within which this view is advanced is valid—namely, that the Corinthians' views and practice had been strongly influenced by Paul himself—the interpretation is neither evident in the passage itself (1 Cor. 1:17—2:5) nor established by reference to 1 Corinthians 14:18, "I thank God that I speak in tongues more than you all."[16] Rather, as the "demonstration of the Spirit and power," Paul referred to the fact that they responded to his preaching with faith.[17] This is the evidence of the power of God, and it is for this reason that he refers back to their conversion. The same moments of reference to his initial ministry and present disagreement occur in Galatians 3:1-5:

O foolish Galatians! Who has bewitched you, before whose eyes Jesus Christ was publicly portrayed as crucified? Let

me ask you only this: Did you receive the Spirit by works
of the law, or by hearing with faith? Are you so foolish?
Having begun with the Spirit, are you now ending with the
flesh? Did you experience so many things in vain?—if it
really is in vain. Does he who supplies the Spirit to you and
works miracles among you do so by works of the law, or by
hearing with faith?

His charge against the Corinthians, like the charge in Galatians
3, is that having begun in the power of God (in the Spirit), they
now think to advance to spiritual perfection on their own. The
terminology in 1 Corinthians is not that of "law"; instead, here
he says "that your faith might not rest in the wisdom of men but
in the power of God" (2:5).

Elsewhere in writing to his converts Paul put great weight
on the conjunction of his preaching and their faith as an authorita-
tive point of reference,[18] and in 1 Thessalonians there are two
statements like those in 1 Corinthians 2:1-5, where again the
reference is to their conversion as evidence that God's power was
present in Paul's initial preaching:

> . . . for our gospel came to you not only in word, but also
> in power and in the Holy Spirit and with full conviction
> (1 Thess. 1:5).
> And we also thank God constantly for this, that when you
> received the word of God which you heard from us, you
> accepted it not as the word of men but as what it really is,
> the word of God, which is at work in you believers (1 Thess.
> 2:13).

To relate the agreement concerning God's power shown in their
response to Paul's preaching to both the present issue and Paul's
application of the word of the cross to that issue, we must notice
how he presented the topic of the modality of possessing God's
gifts. He acknowledged their possession of God's gifts as they
—to assert their claim—acknowledged God's power in his initial
preaching. But Paul now challenges the way in which they understand themselves as possessors of the blessing. An important
element of Paul's argument here, it seems to me, is his reference
to his own conduct of the mission, to his "weakness and . . . much
fear and trembling" when he was with them (1 Cor. 2:3), and
to the theme of imitation, which in 1 Thessalonians occurs in

immediate connection with those references to his initial preaching
which have just been cited (imitation at 1 Thess. 1:6; 2:14) and in
1 Corinthians occurs as a summary of chapters 1-4 (1 Cor. 4:16).[19]

The close similarity of 1 Corinthians and 1 Thessalonians
referred to above and long since noted[20] may require greater
attention than it has recently received, for with the destruction
of the Pauline chronologies based on a synthesis of Acts and
Paul's letters[21] one is restricted to those letters themselves
for determining their relation and hence their sequence, and
this draws greater attention to similarities which the received
chronologies had kept apart, for similarity may imply less
chronological separation. It is symptomatic of this that in
two of the most original attempts to restudy Paul's history,
Hurd's and Schmithals', the Thessalonian letters promise to
play an important role.[22]

The implication of the present consensus concerning 1
Thessalonians should be recognized. If 1 Thessalonians is
the earliest authentic letter by Paul, and intact, then we have
to deal with the fact that it contains two chapters of apparently
unmotivated self-defense, and one feels constrained to conclude that such reference to his mission had already become a favorite theme with Paul. There is no objection to
this in principle, whether the Pauline letters are dated earlier
(with Hurd) or later (with Schmithals), for either allows
time for Paul to have developed the topic and to have given
it a theological interpretation. If that should be the case, then
it could pose considerable difficulty for current efforts to
divine the precise nature of Paul's opponents from his argument, for stereotype could be applied even when not cut
precisely to measure.

However, the current views on the Thessalonian letters
are not as secure as they may seem. There is widespread
agreement that 1 Thessalonians is genuine while 2 Thessalonians is not, and, among those who take both to be genuine,
that the canonical order reflects the order of writing. But the
arguments advanced against the authenticity of 2 Thessalonians are weak. The most impressive—Wrede's argument
from similar statements occurring in the same sequence[23]—
tends, insofar as it is valid at all,[24] to fix on those passages
which make his argument vulnerable to exploitation for
Schmithals' hypothesis that the canonical 1 and 2 Thessalonians are the result of an editorial combination of four
authentic letters to Thessalonica, for those of Wrede's parallels which are most strikingly similar in substance and

sequence read like repetition of the opening and close of a Pauline letter.

Here it is not necessary to try to evaluate the various facets of the matter; it is enough to say that the basis under the current consensus concerning 1 Thessalonians is too fragile to support the inference from that consensus, that Paul's references to his initial mission in 1 Thessalonians were utterly without concrete occasion and so are but stereotyped expressions of one of his favorite themes. My interest here is, however, not to proceed to sift 1 Thessalonians 1-2 for a possible profile of opposition, but to oppose an a priori view that concrete occasion and theological interpretation are mutually exclusive. Paul's statements (in 1 Cor. 1-2) opposing preaching with eloquent words of wisdom may indeed have been due at least in part to criticism directed against rhetorical inadequacies on his part, so that in pleading the power of God he was not a disinterested advocate but was also fighting for his own apostolic authority, identifying his concern with God's concerns; but to say this is not the same as saying that the whole range of this theme in Paul is but an ad hoc self-defense. Hans Conzelmann has presented a persuasive case for the thesis that some of the topics in Paul's letters bear the marks of formulation apart from a concrete occasion which might be deduced from their present position; to account for this he advances the hypothesis of a Pauline school in which theological discussion was fostered as a training in wisdom.[25] This hypothesis thus provides an explanation for the use of pre-formed material in a concrete situation. We must try to understand Paul's references to his initial ministry not just within a concrete situation but also as part of the thought-structure in which Paul asserted the claim that his ministry was a "demonstration of the Spirit and power," for that claim, with its implications and associations, links together much of Paul's thought—on his apostolic authority, his christology, and his understanding of Christian existence.

Their agreement on the demonstration of Spirit and power is the basis of their disagreement, for the question seems to be what *now* constitutes a demonstration of the Spirit and power. In Galatians 2:18 Paul said he would be a transgressor if he re-established what he had torn down, i.e., if he reinstituted the law as the way of salvation; and just following that statement he put the question of the Galatians' current attitude as it related to their initial conversion as a question whether they are now demonstrating God's power or their own: "having begun with the Spirit, are you now ending with the flesh?" (Gal. 3:3). In 1 Corinthians Paul's thoughts are on the same grid, even if the axes are not labeled in terms of the law; the implication of their conversion is "that no human being might boast in the presence of God"; rather, "as it is written, 'Let him who boasts, boast of the Lord' " (1 Cor. 1:29, 31). As the Galatians are charged with attempting to go on to perfection in the flesh, Paul charges the Corinthians with boasting "of men" (1 Cor. 3:21). Neither group verbally denied the power of God in its conversion, but Paul's charge is that the present attitude implies as much: "What have you that you did not receive? If then you received it, why do you boast as if it were not a gift?" (1 Cor. 4:7).

Paul's charge is therefore that the Corinthians' present attitude is not a demonstration of God's power, and they charge him with the same—as is reflected in 2 Corinthians 10-13, and probably we are to infer the same from Paul's references in 1 Corinthians 1-2 to his fear and trembling and to his rejection of eloquence. How is one to discern the spirits here?

IV

To present his own understanding of a mode of possessing God's gifts which is an appropriate demonstration of the Spirit and power, and thus to rebut their understanding, Paul asserted some theological points, the most evident being in eschatology and christology, both being presented in a very *theo*logical perspective. From his eschatology he mocks their assumption that they have arrived and are enriched with the full and final possession of all that God has to give (1 Cor. 4:6-10). His insistence on the eschatological reservation ("already" blessed but not yet exalted out of this life) asserts God's sovereignty and therewith man's historicity, for the Corinthians' reception of God's blessings is not so complete that they are henceforth autonomous vis-à-vis God and consequently also with reference to their neighbors and the world of life *and* death. He contrasts the historicity of the apostles' existence with the Corinthians' assumption of trans-eschatological autonomy:

For I think that God has exhibited us apostles as last of all, like men sentenced to death; because we have become a spectacle to the world, to angels and to men. We are fools for Christ's sake, but you are wise in Christ. We are weak, but you are strong. You are held in honor, but we in disrepute. To the present hour we hunger and thirst, we are ill-clad and buffeted and homeless, and we labor, working with our own hands. When reviled, we bless; when persecuted, we endure; when slandered, we try to conciliate; we have become, and are now, as the refuse of the world, the off-scouring of all things (1 Cor. 4:9-13).

He refers here, among other things, to "weakness" and to "working with our own hands." While it may be that these particular topics were related to specific criticism, here they also have their place in the statement of the full historicity of the apostles' existence.

Historicity is also a weighty part of Paul's christology, since, for all the references to pre-existence, the kenosis is clearly indicated. However one may decide as to the provenance of the various "incarnational" statements,[26] Paul made them his own and used them to assert the historicity of the earthly life of Christ. In making that assertion Paul was interested, as Bultmann rightly observed, "only in the *fact* that Jesus became man and lived on earth. *How* he was born or lived interested him only to the extent of knowing that Jesus was a definite, concrete man . . ."[27] For the statements which some advance as biographical description of the manner of Jesus' earthly life are—wherever the text provides a control—exposition of the kenosis motif or of the death and thus are kerygmatic assertions of concrete historicity rather than being biographical references to Jesus' character and way of life.[28]

Hans Dieter Betz has shown that Paul's call to mimesis is oriented neither to the ethical and moral example of the earthly Jesus, nor to that of the pre-existent Christ, nor to that of Paul, but—as Käsemann said of the hymn in Philippians 2—to the entire saving occurrence itself.[29] For Paul obedient acceptance of the kerygma, to which the mimesis concept calls, was not, as in the mystery religions, an obedience expressed in ritual obligations, but instead finds its expression in the believer's concrete, "secular"

existence, which is no longer dominated by sin but is an enslave-
ment to Christ, occurring concretely in service to one another and
thereby fulfilling the law of Christ which is the requirement of
love.[30] In human life, subject as it is to the dominion of death,
obedient acceptance of the gospel is expressed in a life characterized by mortality, weakness, sickness, oppression, suffering, and,
especially for Paul, the hardships of the apostolic ministry.[31] Paul
emphasized—in distinction from an eternal and ever repeated
myth—the single historical *Dass* of an occurrence which is not to
be repeated, with the consequence that, rejecting a mythical or
miraculous glorification of the reality of human existence, he used
the mimesis concept to urge acceptance of the reality of the
historicity of human existence.[32]

Paul reminded his readers of their conversion as evidence of
the power of God in his preaching, and he referred to his manner
of life—not that weakness, fear, and trembling were religious
gimmicks for calling down the power of God, but, like his reference
to their lowly origins (1 Cor. 1:26-29) and the contrasts between
them and the apostles (1 Cor. 4:9-13)—as an assertion of the
historicity of Christian life, thereby opposing the non-historical
understanding of Christian life held by those in Corinth who
rejected any eschatological reservations, claiming to be filled already, to be enriched, and to be ruling as kings (1 Cor. 4:8).

Throughout his Christian existence the Christian lives *sola
gratia*; he is always to hear the warning, "Let any one who thinks
that he stands take heed lest he fall" (1 Cor. 10:12; cf. Gal.
6:1), for he stands "only through faith," in God's "kindness"
(Rom. 11:20, 22). Those who are mature must, like the apostle,
continue to press on, for they have not already obtained fully
or reached perfection (Phil. 3:12-15). The word of the cross is
the power of God, freeing man from his sinful self-assertion before God, whether that self-assertion be in terms of law or of
wisdom. Like Paul, the Christian is crucified with Christ (Gal.
2:20), crucified to the world (Gal. 6:14), but he is not thereby
glorified out of the world. His existence as a Christian retains its
historicity, its secularity. *Theologia crucis* is a theology not just
for conversion; the word of the cross is the power of God for all
of Christian life.

VI

LAMPADES IN MATTHEW 25:1-13*

Joachim Jeremias

TRANSLATED BY SHIRLEY C. GUTHRIE, JR.

The purpose of this article is to clarify the meaning of the λαμπάδες which the ten virgins carry in Matthew 25:1-13. The question is difficult because the rabbinic sources offer us no help. They tell us that lights were used in wedding processions, but give us no details about the nature of these lights.[1]

Following a centuries-old tradition (which in German-speaking areas was firmly established by Luther's translation), almost all the commentaries translate λαμπάδες with "lamps." The reference in this case would be to the ordinary clay lamps (נֵר plural, נֵרוֹת) which have been found by the thousands in excavations and tombs. Oil lamps were the only kind known in the Palestinian household at the time of Jesus.[2] The probable reason for this traditional interpretation is the reference to oil in verses 3 and 8, and to the flasks of reserve oil in verse 4. This seems applicable only to oil lamps. But the translation "lamps" is certainly wrong. In the first place, there are purely linguistic objections. From the time of the first occurrence of the word in the fifth century before Christ,[3] λαμπάς was consistently used to mean "torch." In the Hellenistic period a wider meaning was given: The λαμπάδες in the palace of Belshazzar,[4] like the λαμπάδες ἀργυραῖ in the splendid tent of Holofernes[5] and in the Egyptian temple,[6] were sconces. That is, they were stands which, like the seven-armed candelabra in the temple of Jerusalem, held several oil lamps. But the interpretation "lamp" can be considered only in isolated cases—as in Acts 20:8, where it is unfortunately not clear whether the reference is not actually to lampstands. It is certain in any case that in the Gospels the word used for oil lamp is λύχνος.[7]

* The original German article was published in *Zeitschrift für die Neutestamentliche Wissenschaft und die Kunde der älteren Kirche* 56, 3/4 (1965), 196-201.

Even more significant than these linguistic objections are the practical objections. Oil lamps were quite unsuited for use outside the house because the slightest breeze would extinguish them. Moreover, their weak light was scarcely bright enough to illuminate the dark out-of-doors. Finally, because they burned a long time,[8] a reserve supply of oil would not have been necessary.

"Lantern" (פַנָס = φανός) cannot be considered as an alternative translation.[9] There is of course reference to them.[10] A nobleman, for instance, always has a servant go before him at night with a lantern.[11] But there is no documentation for this interpretation of λάμπας. Lanterns are called φανοί. Moreover, in John 18:3 they are expressly distinguished from λαμπάδες.

The fact of the matter is that the λαμπάδες mentioned in Matthew 25:1 ff. are *torches* (אֲבוּקָה). This is the usual meaning of the word. This is the way, except in Acts 20:8, it is consistently used in the New Testament. This is the way the parable of the Ten Virgins is depicted in ancient Christian painting and poetry.[12] It is the only interpretation which corresponds to oriental wedding custom.

But how can we reconcile this interpretation with the reference to oil in verses 3, 4, and 8? This mystery was solved by Ludwig Schneller, who as a boy lived in Jerusalem 1858-1864, and served as minister to the Arabian Lutheran Church in Bethlehem 1884-1889. Referring to the Arabian wedding customs of Palestine, he pointed out that we ought not to think of pitch-burning torches; the torches used at evening wedding processions in Bethlehem and vicinity were fed by oil. Schneller describes them as follows: "They are long sticks, around the tops of which are wrapped rags completely soaked with olive oil. A group of girls carry these burning torches in festive procession to the house where the wedding is to take place. There they perform all kinds of dances and figures until the torches go out."[13] This description is not only valid for Bethlehem. G. Dalman observed the same primitive torches (in Arabic *meš'al*, plural *masa 'il*)[14] at evening wedding processions in Ramallah, Dschifna, and El-Kerak.[15] But we have not yet mentioned the decisive point: The torches we have described burn only a very short time—"hardly fifteen minutes"[16]—unless the rags are again soaked with oil.

We may unquestionably assume that the primitive torches used in present-day Arabian Palestine are no different from those used 2,000 years ago. Today also the women who carry the wedding torches are never married women; they are always virgins.[17] It is thus not accidental but in accord with fixed custom that Jesus speaks of παρθένοι in Matthew 25:1, 7, and 11.

II

On the basis of what we have said, several characteristics of the parable of the Ten Virgins appear in a new light. Consider first verse 1b: αἵτινες λαβοῦσαι τὰς λαμπάδας ἑαυτῶν ἐξῆλθον εἰς ὑπάντησιν τοῦ νυμφίου ("who took their torches and went to meet the bridegroom"). Do the girls wait at random just anywhere along the way? Do they wait in an open field? Under trees? At a meeting place previously agreed upon—the entrance to the village, for instance? These suggestions are all forced answers. They are improbable first of all because they think of a village situation, whereas verse 9 (τοὺς πωλοῦντας, "the dealers") suggests a city, there being no bazaars in the villages.[18] On the other hand, it is hard to imagine the resting and sleeping girls in an alleyway of an oriental city.

Even more difficult is a second objection to the usual interpretation that verse 1b refers to a preliminary departure. On the basis of verse 1b (λαβοῦσαι τὰς λαμπάδας ἑαυτῶν) and verse 8 (σβέννυνται, "going out"), this interpretation must presuppose that the ten virgins move out with burning torches. How can that be reconciled with their going to sleep (vs. 5)? Do they go to sleep holding burning torches? And how is it that the torches have not already gone out when the bridegroom arrives? As we have seen, they burn only a short time.

All these difficulties are resolved when we remember that a clear distinction must be made between a parable's introduction and the story itself. All of verse 1, including the subordinate clause in 1b, is only introduction and statement of theme. The subordinate clause gives a closer definition of the ten virgins which is indispensable to the introduction: The following parable intends to describe not just any group of ten girls but a wedding procession. If verse 1b is not a part of the story itself but a part of the statement of theme, then ἐξῆλθον ("they went") in verse 1 refers neither to the girls' march from their houses to meet at the house of the bridegroom, nor to a preliminary departure at random. It refers to the ἐξέρχεσθε ("Come out") in verse 6—to the procession which begins with the coming of the bridegroom at midnight. And verses 2–5 are not a "retrogressive description"[19] which adds to the story what happened before the departure of the girls; these verses are the beginning of the narrative itself. The situation is the same as in Matthew 22:2, where the subordinate clause ὅστις ἐποίησεν γάμους τῷ υἱῷ αὐτοῦ ("who gave a marriage feast for his son") is not the beginning of the narrative but an indispensable part of the introduction to the parable, and where verse 3 is not a retrogressive addition but the beginning of the story.

Now if the ἐξῆλθον in Matthew 25:1b refers to the same event as the ἐξέρχεσθε in verse 6, and if the actual story begins with verse 2, then the description of the situation in verses 2–6 presents no difficulty. The young women have gathered around the bride, and, according to both ancient and modern wedding custom,[20] spend the time talking and dressing the bride. When it seems that the bridegroom is never going to arrive, they go to sleep. Only when they hear the cry announcing his coming do they awake and reach for the torches. Hearing the call to come quickly, the girls put their torches in order (ἐκόσμησαν τὰς λαμπάδας ἑαυτῶν—vs. 7). That is, they pour more oil on the oily rags so that they will burn brightly, and light them. Terrified, some of the girls realize for the first time that they have forgotten to bring the flasks of reserve oil (αγγεῖα— vs. 4). Without more oil, their torches cannot possibly last through the torch dance. If what we have said is correct, their negligence can no longer be judged as lack of foresight excusable by the unexpectedly long delay of the bridegroom. It must be judged as inexcusable, punishable carelessness—just as there is no excuse for the wedding guest in Matthew 22:11 who had not properly cleaned his clothes.

Finally, present-day custom clarifies for the first time the meaning of the phrase in verse 10, εἰσῆλθον μετ' αὐτοῦ εἰς τοὺς γάμους ("they went in with him to the marriage feast"). This does not mean that the wise virgins sit down on the carpets and pillows to eat the wedding feast with the guests. Only the men recline at the table at a feast.[21] The wise virgins enter with the bridegroom and his escort into the courtyard of the wedding house in order to perform the torch dance before the wedding guests until the torches go out.[22]

The main point, however, is that the whole tone of the parable has a new ring when we picture the virgins as a group meeting the bridegroom with blazing torches—not as a group anxiously protecting the tiny flames of little oil lamps which at any moment could be extinguished by the slightest breeze.

III

This parable is one of the parables of crisis. This is immediately apparent from the fact that the story focuses our attention not on the wise but on the foolish virgins. At first, of course, there is a unified picture of a group of young women united in joyous anticipation of the wedding. They are all alike—as are the two men working in the field and the two women grinding at the mill (Matt. 24:40-41; cf. Luke 17:34-35). But a wide gulf suddenly opens up where human eyes can see no distinction, a contrast between life and death. Those on one side are "taken" and those on the other are "left." The first are admitted to the wedding; the others stand before a closed door.

The parable warns of the fate of the foolish virgins. The whole emphasis is on this warning. Why are they excluded? The answer is the same as in the saying about the contemporaries of Noah (Matt. 24:37-39; par. Luke 17:26-27) and of Lot (Luke 17:28-30), and in the parable about the wedding guest with the dirty clothes (Matt. 22:11-13). With inconceivable carelessness and superficiality, all these people have neglected to prepare themselves for the Coming One before the short period of grace runs out.

VII

WORLD IN MODERN THEOLOGY
AND IN NEW TESTAMENT THEOLOGY*
James M. Robinson

Hans-Georg Gadamer prefaces his *Wahrheit und Methode* with
the following quotation from Rilke:

> Solang du Selbstgeworfnes fängst, ist alles
> Geschicklichkeit und lässlicher Gewinn—;
> erst wenn du plötzlich Fänger wirst des Balles,
> den eine ewige Mitspielerin
> dir zuwarf, deiner Mitte, in genau
> gekonntem Schwung, in einem jener Bögen
> aus Gottes grossem Brückenbau:
> erst dann ist Fangen-können ein Vermögen,—
> nicht deines, einer Welt.

> So long as you catch what you yourself have thrown, all is
> skill and justifiable winnings;
> only when you suddenly become the catcher of the ball
> that an eternal playmate
> threw you, dead center, in precisely
> mastered trajectory, in one of those arches
> from God's great bridge-building:
> only then is being able to catch an achievement—
> not your own, a world's.

It seems to me that the common ground of the various new
theologies of our time is a recognition of the problem of theology
as here posed. Surely we vary as to how we each seek to meet this
problem. Indeed, our understandings of the world in terms of which
we gain our skill in catching, and hence our catchings of the ball

* This paper was read at the Colloquium on Theology at Colgate Rochester Divinity
School on September 11, 1967.

themselves, vary considerably. Yet each of the new theologies can be so readily approached in terms of its understanding of world as to suggest that it is in terms of world that theology today is seeking to move beyond a game of solitaire. Consider the ease with which a series of current views of world can be correlated to modern understandings of faith and hence to the major types of theology today: The world is nihilistic and hence faith paradox and theology dialectic. Or: The world is such that God cannot be inferred from its phenomena; faith itself is the phenomenon for theology's inquiry, hence existentialistic interpretation its method. The world is one that has outgrown the mythopoetic age, yet faith is in a mythologically formulated kerygma; hence theology must demythologize to make the kerygma intelligible. Or: The world is secular, come of age; faith no longer has to do with specifically religious τόποι, but rather with the human dilemma as such, what is of ultimate concern; hence theology is to be translated into nonreligious categories and is to affirm secularity as the world for which man has assumed responsibility. Or: World, κόσμος, is not simply the sum total of entities, but rather the way they are made up (κοσμεῖν means to order, arrange, adorn, equip, dress), the way things are structured, the web of meaning in which they are caught, a cultural configuration; world is always a language world, faith not ineffable but a language event, theology hermeneutic. Or: The world is post-Newtonian, not reducible to infinitesimal units of matter, not even to immutable essences or atoms (in the original meaning of ἄτομος: indivisible, unsplittable), but is relativistic, a matter of probabilities, a constantly transmuting process, more like "history" than "nature"; hence theology, while urgently needing liberation from traditional metaphysics, can well build a new metaphysic, including a doctrine of God, upon modern science, which is more congenial to the historic presuppositions of biblical thought than was the Greek ontology that participated in the medieval synthesis. Or: The world has become an atheistic world, which event in our own history is the only catastrophe of modern times really deserving classification as an act of God and the response of commitment appropriate to an act of God—namely, a theology of the death of God. All these portrayals of world are understandings of our world, to which we all, in varying configurations, seem to have turned for skill in catching the ball our late or vivacious playmate aimed our way. I shall seek only to sketch some of what has come my way.

I

MODERN THEOLOGY FROM SCHLEIERMACHER TO BULTMANN

The problem that theology, when it is functioning smoothly, is likely to be the all too facile game of catching on the rebound the ball thrown by oneself, the resubjectivizing of what one has objectified, has been recognized for some time. Hegel sought to escape the egocentric dilemma by appeal to the encounter by the subjective Spirit with the objective Spirit as the absolute Spirit. This position was already challenged by the left-wing Hegelians, who tended to locate the dialectic in matter rather than in Spirit or to infer that the proper object of man's worship was man rather than his deified objectification. But at the collapse of traditional static ontology (with its neat theological potentiality: *natura sive deus*), and the emergence of a historic ontology with its open future, this criticism took on new form; for example, as expressed by Bultmann the year before Rilke's death.

> . . . The idealistic observer sees nothing in history that can lay a claim on him in the sense that here something new is said to him that he does not already potentially possess and have at his disposal by means of his participation in reason in general. He finds nothing that encounters him as authority, he finds in history only himself, in that the content of history is reduced to the movement of ideas coordinated to man's rationality. Thus all along he has at his disposal all possibilities of historic occurrence.[1]

If, then, idealism's appeal to history did not transcend the confines of boomerang theology, recourse has since been taken to theology oriented to the future, where what comes is new and contingent, hence potentially at least not just a game of solitaire but real encounter, conceivably even with a God other than oneself. Faith is eschatological existence. Yet the kingdoms of this world have not been replaced by the kingdom of our God and his Christ, the eschaton has not come, the parousia has been delayed, the world is too much with us for faith to be the flight of the alone to the alone. We seem to be permanently between the times. If man is the historic animal, then he is the product of heredity and environment as well as being continually constituted anew by decision or encounter.

The structures for thinking such faith were provided to Bultmann by Heidegger's analysis of *Dasein*; for example, in the reciprocity of *Geworfenheit* and *Entwurf,* terms whose etymological affinity to each other and to Rilke's figure of the thrown ball is somewhat obscured in the standard translation "thrownness" and "projection," where different etymological roots are employed. The point in using one root for the two terms is that when man in his ontological freedom projects his being, this projection is always in terms of his givenness, his facticity, his thrownness.

> The projection of its (sc. *Dasein's*) ownmost potentiality-for-Being has been delivered over to the Fact of its thrownness into the "there."[2]

It is this dialectic reciprocity or balance between thrownness and projection that inheres in being in the world. Hence Heidegger can define *Dasein* as "thrown projection," "thrown projective Being-in-the-world."[3]

Thus Bultmann's transcending of history in favor of eschatology, of essence in favor of existence, so as to transcend the solitaire of "historicism" (which he recognized as no more than "psychologism" writ large), was not a return to individualism or mysticism, but rather a conceptual structuring in which, to use traditional (though no longer really applicable) terminology, "anthropology" ("understanding of existence") was projected upon as well as projecting "cosmology" ("understanding of world"). Hence Bultmann defines the theological task in quite balanced form as consisting of "unfolding that understanding of God, and hence of the world and man, which arises from faith."[4]

Yet this dialectic balance is tipped slightly. Heidegger has said in the same context:

> Understanding *can* devote itself primarily to the disclosedness of the world; that is, *Dasein* can, proximally and for the most part, understand itself in terms of its world. Or else understanding throws itself primarily into the "for-the-sake-

of-which"; that is, *Dasein* exists as itself. Understanding is
either authentic, arising out of one's own Self as such, or
inauthentic.[5]

To be sure, Heidegger goes on to point out that this tipping of
the balance does not actually transcend the conceptual structure.

> The "in-" of "inauthentic" does not mean that *Dasein* cuts
> itself off from its Self and understands "only" the world.
> The world belongs to Being-one's-Self as Being-in-the-world.
> On the other hand, authentic understanding, no less than
> that which is inauthentic, *can* be either genuine or not
> genuine.[6]

Also without transcending that theoretical structure, Bultmann
nonetheless tipped the balance in (Pauline) theology in an analogous way.

> Every assertion about God is simultaneously an assertion
> about man and vice versa. For this reason and in this sense
> Paul's theology is, at the same time, anthropology. But since
> God's relation to the world and man is not regarded by Paul
> as a cosmic process oscillating in eternally even rhythm, but
> is regarded as constituted by God's acting in history and by
> man's reaction to God's doing, therefore every assertion
> about God speaks of what He does with man and what He
> demands of him. And, the other way around, every assertion
> about man speaks of God's deed and demand—or about man
> as he is qualified by the divine deed and demand and by his
> attitude toward them. The christology of Paul likewise is
> governed by this point of view. In it, Paul does not specula-
> tively discuss the metaphysical essence of Christ, or his
> relation to God, or his "natures," but speaks of him as the one
> through whom God is working for the salvation of the world
> and man. Thus, every assertion about Christ is also an as-
> sertion about man and vice versa; and Paul's christology is
> simultaneously soteriology.
>
> Therefore, Paul's theology can best be treated as his
> doctrine of man ...[7]

However, the role of Heidegger's conceptual structure in Bultmann's theology may in this case be not simply that of suggesting
such a tilt, but rather that of reassuring Bultmann that, with the
positive contribution Heidegger had made to the understanding
of man as historic, such a tilt could be carried through without the

loss of world, history, and God, hence without regression to subjectivism and individualism. For Bultmann's tilt actually carries out on Heideggerian terms what Schleiermacher had envisaged on romantic terms but not dared to carry through. For Bultmann's organization of theology in terms of an understanding of existence is in effect the carrying out of Schleiermacher's ultimate intention, whereas the new hermeneutic is intended to rectify this tilt.

A year before the publishing of the second edition of *The Christian Faith,* Schleiermacher published in his second open letter to Lücke a statement of how he would like to have reorganized his book.[8] His first *desideratum*[9] was to reverse the order of his two main divisions, so as to begin with man's need of salvation and the doctrine of Christ as Savior, and only then present his doctrine of God. That is to say, he would have liked to follow the sequence anthropology, soteriology, christology, theology. For he would hope in this way to bring to an end the "complete misunderstanding" "that my dogmatics is really philosophy."[10] Now this sequence is not only that of the Heidelberg Catechism, to which Schleiermacher, himself in the Reformed tradition, refers, but also that of Bultmann's Pauline theology, with the exception that Bultmann not only begins with Paul's anthropological terminology, but also uses "man" as the overarching category of his outline: "Man Prior to the Revelation of Faith" and "Man under Faith,"[11] much as Schleiermacher in fact uses "the pious self-consciousness" (1) as "presupposed" (apart from the human contradiction) and (2) "as determined by the contradiction."

Schleiermacher's second *desideratum*[12] is introduced as follows:

Indeed I have seriously reflected whether already in this second edition of my book it is not time for another reworking of it with regard to its structuring. I have in mind that structure which is already hinted at and almost promised, in that the two forms of dogmatic assertions, those which express attributes of God and those which express characteristics of the world, are called only secondary forms. For if it is true that they express nothing that in its essential substance is not contained in statements that the basic form embraces—

then both the other forms can be dispensed with. And that is indeed my conviction, to which is related also the conviction that our doctrine of faith will some day learn to get along without them.[13]

Schleiermacher did not carry out this revision, for he felt that the original format provided a better "point of contact"[14] for his polemic against the way doctrine was being currently presented in the church. But, just as he "consoled himself" in the case of the first *desideratum* with the assurance "that sooner or later another will come to carry through with enthusiasm and success this vastly superior arrangement"[15] just so with regard to the second *desideratum* he looks to "the upcoming generation." "In any case I rejoice in the conviction that I have at least seen from a distance the form of a freer and more lively way of treating our doctrine of faith."[16]

These *desiderata* are not passing whims on Schleiermacher's part, but emerge from the basic structure of his theological system; hence it would not be surprising, in view of the influence he had on subsequent theology, to find them being carried out, even if in the intellectual context of a later age.

Schleiermacher's point of departure had been his definition of the essence of piety, "by which it is distinguished from all other feelings," as "this, that we are conscious of ourselves as absolutely dependent, or, what is intended to say the same thing, as in relation with God."[17] In his first open letter to Lücke in 1829[18] he explained that he does not envisage "unconscious feelings," nor does he wish to speak of self-consciousness as "knowledge." Rather religion is more like the "attitude" (*Gesinnung*) pervading all one's knowing, acting, and feeling.[19]

Apparently Schleiermacher had in mind something like what Jakob Friedrich Fries in 1805 distinguished from "feeling" as a religious *a priori sui generis,* termed *Ahndung* (cf. modern German *Ahnung,* meaning dim awareness, intuition, sensitivity, faint glimmering). Fries's view was picked up by de Wette and then revived a century later by Rudolf Otto[20] and Wilhelm Bousset.[21] This "Neo-Friesianism"[22] was Bultmann's philosophy-of-religion context until 1922. Symptomatic of this orientation were his role as mystagogue in the conjuring of the numinous in a session of the

"Michelchen cult" in 1922, described by Karl Barth in *Revolutionary Theology in the Making;*[23] his involvement in the publication of the posthumous edition of Bousset's *Kyrios Christos,* 1921, acknowledged in the preface;[24] and his making sense of the second edition of Barth's *Romans* as a philosophy of religion comparable to Schleiermacher's *Discourses on Religion,* Otto's *Idea of the Holy,* and "modern attempts to demonstrate a religious *a priori.*"[25] To be sure, Bultmann at that time shifted to dialectic theology, renounced the concept of a religious *a priori,* and became Otto's opponent at Marburg. Yet Wilhelm Herrmann's distinction between the path to faith as faith's indispensable ground, on the one hand, and the thoughts faith engenders as *adiaphora,* on the other hand, had a continuing influence on Bultmann. The result was that Schleiermacher's "self-consciousness," interpreted as *Ahndung,* then as the Herrmannian experience that grounds faith—"experience" meant not psychologically but existentialistically (cf. *Anfange der dialektischen Theologie,* I, 121)—became Bultmann's "self-understanding," whose dispensable objectification is myth.

For Schleiermacher—and for Bultmann—all subdivisions within theology seem to be in theory equally external to religion. When Schleiermacher emphasizes that piety is independent of conceptualizations, he can list alongside the "idea of God" among such conceptualizations also the "idea of freedom";[26] and among "statements on the characteristics of the world" that can be made on the basis of natural science without religion he can include "all statements of generally anthropological content."[27] Anthropology as idea has no priority over theology and cosmology. Similarly Bultmann can begin his essay on demythologizing by listing, among the aspects of the outmoded mythical world-view, not only cosmological but also anthropological views. To this extent anthropology has for Schleiermacher and Bultmann no priority over theology or cosmology, in that all are ideas and hence derivative, since "the statements are what is only derived, whereas the inner frame of mind (*Gemüthszustand*) is what is primal."[28] Schleiermacher classifies all such statements either "as descriptions of aspects of human life (*Lebenszustände*), or as concepts of divine attributes and actions, or as expressions of characteristics of the world."[29] All three forms of statements would seem according to his system to be in theology equally derivative, in that all may be derived from the "higher self-consciousness," the "feeling of absolute dependence," the "consciousness of being in relation to God," the religious "frame of mind."

Yet in describing in detail (in par. 30) the three forms of statements, Schleiermacher refers to the first as itself "descriptions of frames of mind" (*Gemüthszustände*), so that in terminology the religious ("inner") experience itself and the first derivative conceptualization of it are directly coordinated. In Schleiermacher's view this closer relationship is justified by the fact that the first form of statement can *only* be derived from "inner experience," whereas the second form *could* be derived from metaphysics, the third from natural science. Hence the first form is the "basic form," whereas the second and third are admissible only when derived from religious experience, or, as Schleiermacher more precisely put it, "to the extent they can be developed out of statements of the first form" (*ibidem*). It is understandable that he refers to them as "secondary" or "peripheral" forms,[30] which could well be dispensed with.

The "subsequent future" to which Schleiermacher "entrusts" this mission[31] would seem to have arrived less with the "upcoming generation" (though one might think of Kierkegaard) than with Bultmann. Bultmann's historic rather than individualistic understanding of the self should have distinguished his term "self-understanding" from subjectivism. His equivalent term "understanding of existence" even stands in etymological affinity to "ecstasy," being "out of oneself." Heidegger himself presents a nonsubjective interpretation of what *Existenz* in *Sein und Zeit* meant,[32] and he associated "man's ek-sistence" with "the ecstatic character of *Da-sein*."[33] All this should have made clear Bultmann's presupposition of the temporality of being. Yet the subjectivistic misunderstanding did take place, in no less distinguished quarters than Karl Barth.[34] For he here criticizes Bultmann to the effect that theological statements, since they have to do with the God who *encounters* man, "are not to be reduced to statements about man's inner life." To this Bultmann responded:

The last sentence betrays complete misunderstanding of what existentialistic interpretation, and the meaning attached to existence in it, is. This is not the "inner life of man" at all, which can be brought under observation while setting aside what is different from it and what it encounters (whether environment, fellow-man or God)—say from a view which has to do with psychology of religion, but at all events not from an existentialistic one. For the latter seeks to contemplate and to understand the real (historic) existence of man, who exists only in a living connection with what is "different" from him—only in encounters. And existentialistic analysis is concerned with the relevant terminology in which that might occur. Barth obviously orientates his views of it on a concept of anthropology taken from Feuerbach, and ascribes this to Wilhelm Herrmann, instead of seeing that Herrmann is struggling (even if he does so with an inadequate terminology) to comprehend human being as historic.[35]

Nonetheless the original Cartesian overtone in the term "self" has continued to drown out its redefinition by Bultmann, and he has had to repeat his correction,[36] just as I have sought to defend my use of his terminology from the same misunderstanding.[37] Indeed, Bultmann makes the same criticism of modern religiosity which, on the basis of that misunderstanding, is made of him. "In (modern) religiosity precisely that is given up which—at least according to the Christian faith—grounds genuine religion: the tie-in of man to the transcendent God as standing over against him (*Gegenüber*). Religiosity has been thought out from (the point of view of) the subjectivity of man."[38]

In view of the fact that the redefinition of "self" in terms of the temporality of man continues to be drowned out by the subjectivism that is an aspect of the fate of the Cartesian world, there has been a trend toward replacing the term "self-understanding" not only with the slightly less misleading term "understanding of existence," but with such circumlocutions as "understanding of the present,"[39] "understanding of time,"[40] and "understanding of reality."[41]

This corresponds to a development in the understanding of language in the new hermeneutic that seeks to rectify the tilt in a way analogous to Rilke's formulation: "a power—not your own, a world's." Rather than primarily man's ex-pression, language is world's mode of being. This rectification corresponds also to a rectification of the standard interpretation of Schleiermacher's hermeneutic derived from Dilthey, or, more precisely, the detection behind the later Schleiermacher's position, which is all that had been accessible thus far, of a position in his early hermeneutical writings that is less affected by that tilt, in that originally the given epoch's style stood more in balance with the individual's expression.

> Schleiermacher's most personal contribution in the process was the psychological interpretation, according to which each thought of a text, as a moment from life, must be reflected back upon the personal context of its author's life, if it is to be fully understood. Meanwhile we have gained a somewhat more exact insight into the history of the emergence of Schleiermacher's thoughts on hermeneutic, now that the Berlin manuscripts from which Lücke back then composed his edition have been published in an accurate copy by the Heidelberg Academy of Sciences. The outcome of this recourse to the original manuscripts is not revolutionary, but yet not without significance. H. Kimmerle shows in his Introduction how the first sketches give prominence to the identity of thinking and speaking, while the later expansion sees in speaking the individualizing expression. In addition there is the slow emergence and ultimate domination by the psychological viewpoint over the genuinely linguistic viewpoints of "technical" interpretation ("style").[42]

This drift toward subjectivism in Schleiermacher's understanding of language is symptomatic of a more pervasive cultural drift into subjectivism from the 18th to the 19th century, which Gadamer[43] exemplified with the term "expression," which originally was used more in the sense of finding the right expression to communicate the intended meaning or produce the desired effect than in the sense of bringing out one's own inner experience. One sought the right "expression" in the sense of seeking the language that preserved truth's stamp or imprint upon it uncorrupted, so as to transfer the original "impression" to the hearer.

If then language is not necessarily or basically ex-pression as an objectification of some ontologically more primal experience or dimension of man's being, but rather the being of world taking place, then the task of theology in interpreting religious language would not be completed in stating the frame of mind or understanding of existence that it secondarily formulated or objectified as characteristics of the world and attributes of God, or as myth; rather, theology's task is to recognize that religious language bears the imprint of God's world upon it and hence to explicate faith not only in terms of the believer but first of all in terms of his world as God's world.

This does not mean a return to a traditional compartmentalized theology, or to cosmological and metaphysical speculations of faith, as Schleiermacher feared. Hence it does not mean a revival of the "secondary" or "peripheral" forms in their original structure as *loci* alongside of anthropology. Rather the point of departure for the advance is the recognition, accompanying the tilt envisaged by Schleiermacher and carried out in existentialistic interpretation, that the "basic form" or "understanding of existence" contains already an awareness or understanding of world and God as well as man. Schleiermacher was able to understand "the pious feeling" as "the primal expression of an unmediated existentialistic relation,"[44] i.e., "to the extent that the relation between the world and God is expressed therein."[45] Hans Jonas anticipated demythologization with a philosophic analysis to the effect that "what is basic and at the same time specific in a given concretion of *Dasein* consists in its *relation* to the world—its world—and to itself, . . . [which] takes place as understanding of being."[46] Bultmann in the essay of 1941 proposing demythologization began his demythologized presentation of "man's being apart from faith" with an analysis of the "dialectic relation" of "this world" to "the world as God's creation"; and his presentation of "man's being in faith" begins with an analysis of "deworldifying."[47] Thus it is the presence of the totality of theology in the "basic" form that has been obscured—partly by the anthropocentric cast given theology, partly by the "subjectivistic" misunderstanding of modern theology by its critics—and that now needs to be clearly grasped. Once this is clearly seen, this "basic" form is not only vindicated, but also freed from the necessity of being focused in terms of man. Faith can be interpreted "existentialistically" in terms of world; indeed, the language of faith is to be understood basically as bringing God's world to language.

II

NEW TESTAMENT THEOLOGY
FROM APOCALYPTICISM TO GNOSTICISM

It is this shift, this rectification of the tilt in the balance, that I would like to exemplify in terms of a direction for New Testament theology beyond Bultmann. However, before entering into such a suggestion, it is relevant to draw attention to the extent to which the rectification itself can be regarded as a possibility latent in Bultmann's own orientation to New Testament research, which after all is responsible for replacing the individual author or life with the *Sitz im Leben* of the community as the legitimate orientation of kerygmatic theology. To be sure, Bultmann did not separate Jesus' word from his person, but rather regarded the understanding of existence coming to expression in that word not only as an offer of that understanding to the hearer (thus anticipating Gadamer's positive interpretation of "expression"), but also as bringing out the way Jesus understood his own existence (from which understanding of language as ex-pression the later Heidegger distanced himself), as I have shown in some detail in the second edition of *Kerygma und historischer Jesus*[48] over against the contrary interpretation by Van A. Harvey and Schubert M. Ogden.[49] Yet Bultmann did not assume that language expresses existence to the exclusion of world. "If man's being is historic, it is inherent in it that in his thinking man opens up his world and his existence and in his talking shares them with others."[50] Indeed, in the first theoretical statement of a demythologizing hermeneutic, Hans Jonas already rectified the tilt in a way reminiscent of Rilke.

> That upon which this reversion (sc. back from objectification to existentialistic terrain) strikes, that which the dismantling process produces as the existential basis, does not in this process need to be taken as an individual, biographical fact, e.g. about Augustine or any other author. In the symbolistic and rational accessibility that the dogma provides, the mere

symbolic-conceptual formula can be very well discussed, and indeed on the plane of the most rigorous theoretical stringency, without the originative phenomena having yet been carried out existentialistically, or having really been experienced personally by the author in question or even by his whole generation. Then the task of the hermeneutical reversion refers precisely to the real author, namely the historical totality of *Dasein* (*Gesamtdasein*), which, reaching beyond individuals and generations, has produced this interpretation of itself, of its most intimate (being), and in it preserved itself for a whole epoch of human history, as a mode, perhaps often only latent or conventionally buttressed, yet always actualizable, of the capacity for being that in fact is accessible to it alone. It is only this "history-of-ideas subject" as such that philosophic hermeneutic has in view.[51]

If Bultmann oriented his Pauline theology to anthropology, it was in part at least because he thought Paul's theology derives from anthropology;[52] in his Johannine theology Bultmann approaches the matter in terms of the Johannine understanding of the world. Nevertheless, in both cases the presentation culminated in terms of eschatological existence. Such existence is also the norm on the basis of which other theologies in the New Testament and the Apostolic Fathers are evaluated, thus functioning as the organizing theological principle of his whole *Theology of the New Testament*. It is for the sake of this orientation to an understanding of existence that Pauline and Johannine theology are arranged in a systematic rather than historical outline, and indeed that the sequence of different theologies in early Christianity (e.g., in Chapter VII, "The Core of the Development") is less in terms of their relationships in the history of ideas than in terms of the ascending and descending levels in the rise and fall of an understanding of existence.

To a certain extent the procedure of arranging New Testament theology in terms of material relationships (however these may be formulated) rather than historical continuities was the appropriate inference from the state of things with regard to continuity and discontinuity in the history of ideas within early Christianity as it has presented itself to historical analysis in Bultmann's time. Pauline theology cannot be derived from Jesus' teaching.[53] Mark can be derived neither from Jesus[54] nor from Paul.[55] Nor can

Luke be derived from Paul.[56] Not only can John not be derived from Jesus (Ferdinand Christian Baur), it cannot even be derived from the Synoptics;[57] nor can John be derived from Paul.[58] The book of Revelation is cut off from the Fourth Gospel, and Hebrews from Paul and his school. No New Testament author can be explained in terms of contact with the historical Jesus, and less than half the New Testament was composed during the generation of the original disciples (i.e., prior to A.D. 70). The threads of continuity in the history of ideas are lost, and the gaping chasms of discontinuity confronting the scholar invite some other organizing principle for New Testament theology than that of discernible relationships between authors in the history of ideas. As Franz Overbeck put it, the primitive Christian writings are "pre-historic." Bultmann did what he could under such circumstances, pooling all resources to provide an anonymous context of early Christian theology under such categories as "The Kerygma of the Earliest Church," "The Kerygma of the Hellenistic Church Aside from Paul," and "The Development toward the Ancient Church." But even such an anonymous context in the history of Hellenistic religious ideas does not make intelligible the emergence of what for Bultmann is decisive in primitive Christianity: a definitive understanding of existence in Paul and John that peters out in the Apostolic Fathers. For the causal relationships in the history of ideas is not the dimension in which the dynamics of understandings of existence become intelligible. But the history of world *is,* and hence the great importance for historical understanding that is to be attached to casting New Testament theology upon the trajectory of the understanding of world in the Hellenistic age.

The initial hermeneutical steps to be taken to surmount the limitations of a historical methodology that merely juxtaposes the history of religious ideas with relatively unrelated understandings of existence can be inferred from the following example, Gunther Gawlick's review[59] of Ulrich Wilcken's monograph *Weisheit und Torheit: Eine exegetisch-religionsgeschichtliche Untersuchung zu 1. Kor. 1 und 2.*[60] Gawlick summarizes Wilcken's treatment of Stoicism as follows:

> The rival movements in Late Antiquity (Christianity, Gnosticism and Stoicism, the last standing for all the schools of

Hellenistic philosophy) each and all meet in a basic existential experience, which one can describe as *loss of world*. Classical Greece's confidence in being had articulated itself in the concept *cosmos*. For Hellenism and Late Antiquity, on the other hand, *world* means first of all a confusing plurality of objects that arouse in the subject a feeling of being threatened, and the resultant need for security and salvation. . . . The Stoic system is, according to the author's view, one of the various attempts to overcome this dilemma. This is what makes it possible to compare Stoic philosophy in structure and intention with Gnosticism, and to regard both as met by Paul's polemic in 1 Cor. 1-2. The Stoic system, like the Gnostic one, derives from the "basic experience of the insecurity of one's own being among the beings" (p. 254), as the answer to a "primal, eternal threat" (p. 239).

Gawlick's criticism of such a historical analysis is derived from his recognition of the hermeneutical relevance of language in history.

The author abstracts completely from the varying *historical conditions* under which Stoicism and Gnosticism articulate their basic experience. But all thought stands under the necessity, in explicating its basic experience, of making use of a conceptual apparatus which is not created anew whenever one sees fit, but in part is taken over from the context of some other experience. . . . It is clear that the classical Greek concept "cosmos" was not discontinued by Alexander's death. It seems precisely in Stoicism to have developed a distinctive after-effect. *Zeno of Kition* infers from the *perfection* of the world that it must possess reason, understanding and soul, i.e. predicates of God (*SVF*, I, 111). This "proof of God" does not fit well the interpretation that the author (Wilckens) gives to Stoic philosophy: If Stoicism derives only from an experience in which beings must first be mastered before world can come together as cosmos, then Stoicism cannot build *a priori* upon the perfection of the world. . . . The illustrations make it clear that concepts do not without further ado stand at the disposal of an experience as submissive instruments of articulation. Rather concepts must be taken over together with their historical webs, which then work over into their new area of activity, and can explode the monolithic unity of a system. Every attempt to explain a philosophy only from a basic experience has here its inescapable limitation.

Not only does the available language condition the philosophic explication of a basic experience (Gawlick's point); it also conditions the experience itself, as the experience of persons for whom language is constitutive of their being. With regard to New Testament theology, this means that the major focus for the next generation lies neither in a return to the effort to recover the lost threads of continuity in the history of ideas from author to author nor in the unrelated juxtaposition of converging or diverging understandings of existence (although ongoing research in both dimensions will play a part in any future synthesis of significance), but in the tracing of world as it comes into language. For in this movement one can trace the historical trajectory to which understandings of existence can be meaningfully related and hence historically interpreted.

One such trajectory is that from Jewish apocalypticism to Christian Gnosticism, with which I wish to illustrate briefly what is involved. Even in the history of ideas there is some continuity from apocalypticism to Gnosticism. With the concreteness given to Jewish apocalypticism by Qumran, a dualistic trend (e.g., "light" vs. "darkness," "flesh" vs. "spirit") and an emerging prominence of "knowing" can be seen to point toward emergent Gnosticism. For although the ultimate origins of Gnosticism are still not clear, one can now recognize Gnosticism emerging as an artful and artificial myth (*Kunstmythos*) in the Hellenistic age.[61] The Gnostic redeemer myth is, however, not in origin a perversion of christology, not a Christian heresy in essence. The leading recent advocate of that view, Carsten Colpe,[62] has given up that position and now recognizes[63] that in Manicheism and Mandeism the myth developed parallel to Christianity, and in the cases of Simon Magus and the Hymn of the Pearl may have existed in kernel prior to Christianity. Hence it is in origin a non-Christian phenomenon, as the Coptic Gnostic library found near Nag Hammadi makes evident. For one non-Christian Gnostic treatise, "The Letter of Eugnostos the Blessed," is also present in a Christianized form as "The Sophia of Jesus Christ," thus providing a model of the way in which a non-Christian Gnostic tractate could be cut up and edited into question and answer form so as to become a

Christian Gnostic dialogue of the Resurrected with his disciples. The same situation is conjectured to be present in other Nag Hammadi tractates that survive only in Christian Gnostic form, such as "The Apocryphon of John," "The Hypostasis of the Archons," "The Book of Thomas the Athlete," and "The Acts of Peter and the Twelve Apostles."[64]

This non-Christian Gnosticism of Nag Hammadi is in several cases not non-Jewish; to be sure, as Hans Jonas insists,[65] it is at best apostate-Jewish—yet in any case it found in Jewish lore, especially the book of Genesis, its quarry of materials. Now two apparently non-Christian "Jewish" Gnostic tractates that are represented at Nag Hammadi only in their non-Christian form reflect in their background Jewish apocalypticism. The "Apocalypse of Adam" is a revelation not only in the general sense that it is Adam's testament recounting the future to Seth (Genesis thrown with a curve), but also in the sense that it culminates in a still future description of final conflict and the conversion of the nations. And the "Paraphrase of Shem" refers to coming earthquakes, famines, and blasphemies, culminating in the final destruction of the whole world. Now these apocalyptic tractates can hardly be called pre-Gnostic, for their apocalypticism has gnosticizing aspects and each contains its version of the Gnostic redeemer myth. Hence it would be more accurate to say that we have to do with sources documenting a transition from traditionally apocalyptic to Gnostic casts given to Jewish apocalyptic language patterns.

Such a change in cast within a continuing linguistic tradition involves of course linguistic changes themselves, which, though at first almost imperceptible, gradually come to attention as a shift in world that can ultimately break language patterns, with such a result as the ultimately non-apocalyptic form into which Gnosticism tended to develop. Such a gradual change in cast emerging within a language tradition is what is meant by a "trajectory." New Testament theology is not to be conceived of as resting upon a fixed "background," as is implied in such a standard phrase as "the Jewish background of the New Testament," but is rather to be conceived of as caught up in such trajectories. One such trajectory, that from Jewish apocalypticism to "Jewish" Gnosticism, took place without noticeable influence from Christianity, but was itself a matrix in which primitive Christianity moved and in terms of which the history of primitive Christian theology is in part to be understood. This trajectory was one significant aspect not only of the history of ideas, but also of the history of world in early Christianity.

Perhaps the Gnostic Christian claim to be the truly apostolic Christianity reflects some awareness of the continuity within this trajectory of world. Put conversely, the Gnostic Christian criticism of the orthodox Christianity of the second century as apostate, for example in its distinction between "gnostics" and "pistics," may reflect some awareness of the emergence of a more worldly world within the Early Catholic Church. The Christian criticism of Gnosticism cannot legitimately ignore the shift in world in the move from primitive to orthodox Christianity; that is to say, a valid criticism of Gnosticism would not be necessarily identical with a vindication of the Early Catholic Church. Rather, a valid Christian criticism of Gnosticism must investigate the shift in cast that "loss of world" underwent on the trajectory from Jewish apocalypticism to Christian Gnosticism; it should seek to identify within the altering language patterns the Gnostic defection from the substance of primitive Christianity. The "loss of world" in primitive Christianity's expectation of the "imminent end of the world" was a different "world" both from the Qumranian apocalyptic withdrawal from the world and from the "loss of world" in Gnostic Christianity's otherworldly escapism.

From a purely formal point of view both versions of "loss of world" on the trajectory from Jewish apocalypticism to Christian Gnosticism were "world," just as much as was the more "worldly" world of the Jewish establishment in Jerusalem and its successors after the fall of Jerusalem, normative Judaism and orthodox Christianity. For the materially loaded formulations "loss of world" and "worldly" are language called forth each from the viewpoint of an opposing world. From the viewpoint of the classical concept of an ordered *kosmos* informed by reason or God, the world of apocalypticism and primitive Christianity could only be looked upon privately, as a-cosmic, i.e., as "loss of world."

From the apocalyptic, primitive Christian, or Gnostic point of view, the Jewish establishment, normative Judaism, and the Early Catholic Church could only be regarded as succumbing to "this present evil aeon," "this world"; i.e., as "worldly." From a purely formal point of view all these conflicting points of view were oriented to an understanding of world and hence are to be understood in terms of "world"; in such a purely formal sense none has lost world, none is more "worldly," more characterized by world, than another.

It is in terms of these trajectories from apocalyptic to Gnostic "loss of world" and from "loss of world" to "worldly" that the history of New Testament theology is to be traced. Paul is located somewhere in the middle of the trajectory from apocalypticism to Gnosticism. Both forms of loss of world are involved in his theology, with an apocalyptic conviction that the form of this world is passing away and a Gnostic view that the evil spirit-world rulers could not recognize the redeemer whom they crucified. Paul's problems in his churches had to do largely with excesses of both kinds of loss of world, from the excessive apocalypticism at Thessalonica that was not prepared for death prior to the parousia, to the gnosticizing rejection at Corinth of bodily resurrection as superfluous once one had been initiated. Paul reassured the Thessalonians that the new world coming with the parousia would include the dead and argued to the otherworldly Corinthians that relations in the world—represented by the body —continued to be relevant in this life and the world to come (resurrected body).

To be sure, the most violent opposition to Paul came from a more worldly direction, both the Judaizers who did not want to upset the Palestinian establishment and the miracle-working Jewish-Christian missionaries who invaded Corinth at the time of Second Corinthians and sought to discredit Paul for not having the imposing credentials of the successful holy man of the day. Paul met the Judaizers with the doctrine of justification independent of man's work in the world and the miracle-workers with an unworldly indifference to achievements in this world, even to knowing the earthly Jesus. It was this potentially gnosticizing side of Paul which his school heard as his "world"; hence Colossians moved clearly one step beyond Paul, replacing the apocalyptic with the Gnostic version of loss of world; for example, in transferring the believer's exit from the world of darkness back into the present, with his resurrection life already hidden in heaven and the future only bringing an anticlimactic revelation of that already possessed heavenly life denuded of all apocalyptic trappings. Ephesians goes even further into the Gnostic world; yet there is here a Qumranian admixture, not of apocalypticism, but rather of the liturgical cadence of the Hodayoth and the order's stress upon the unity of the group, thus providing an uneasy merger of Gnostic world and emergent orthodoxy, as one also finds in Ignatius of Antioch. But this uneasy merger polarizes in the next generation of Paulinists. There is a clearly Gnostic wing, to which the Gnostic heresiarchs of the early second century such as Valentinus and Basilides appeal for their Paulinism. Their case is contested by the orthodox Paulinist Pastoral Epistles and Acts, in which a Christian establishment takes over, with a more worldly world pointing toward Bishop Callistus in Rome one century later and to Constantine another century later, just as the Gnostic Paulinists pointed to Marcion and the Christian Gnosticism of the subsequent centuries.

A different stream of primitive Christianity had begun with Q, also in a world in transition from apocalypticism to Gnosticism. This collection of sayings without narrative sounded increasingly disembodied, with the Gospel of Thomas as the logical outcome, an outcome blocked by nascent orthodoxy tying Q down to earth by means of the narrative framework of Matthew and Luke, which they had borrowed from Mark. Incidentally, this move played down the aura of mystery Mark had superimposed upon the all too worldly narrative tradition behind him. This more worldly narrative tradition is represented by the miraculous "Miracles Source" behind John, which John spiritualized with discourses out of this world, composed in affinity to nascent Gnosticism's loss of world. John was first popular in Gnostic circles, but finally was rescued for orthodoxy by Irenaeus, perhaps thanks to an ecclesiastic redactor.

Thus the trajectories along which primitive Christianity's history can be plotted are discernible in terms of the history of "world," which took place in the transition from "loss of world," which had its being in the language of apocalypticism transmuted into Gnosticism, into worldliness, which had its being in the Jewish establishment which was succeeded after the fall of Jerusalem by normative Judaism and orthodox Christianity. Of course individual texts and movements within primitive Christianity represent various ways of modulating the overriding trajectories in which they were caught up, in which individual freedom and creativity within history come to expression. Yet the history of primitive Christianity is not only or even primarily the expression of the religious experience of individuals or the objectification of their understandings of existence, but rather the history of world, from apocalyptic loss of world to Gnostic loss of world or to worldliness. This history of world is the transcendental dimension of the history of primitive Christianity, and hence its investigation the prerequisite to a more adequate understanding of what was really happening.

It is in terms of this history of world that the other forms of theology—namely, the understanding of existence and an analogous doctrine of God—come into historical focus. It is the shift in world on the part of the type of Christianity that won out, the shift from "loss of world" toward "worldly," that is at work in the petering out of eschatological existence. And it is that shift in world which projects the Pauline "god of this world" (2 Cor. 4:4) and Johannine "ruler of this world" (John 12:31; 14:30; 16:11) from the status of hostile categories alongside the benevolent God the Father into *de facto* absorption *in bonam partem* into the Creator and Cosmocrator on the part of orthodoxy and, in reaction, into *de jure* identification *in malem partem* with the previously ineffable Yahweh as the now defamed Yaldabaoth on the part of Gnosticism. Theology is not to be analyzed as having a "basic form" and two "peripheral forms," an "existentialistic" formulation and mythological objectifications. Rather one should recognize in what Schleiermacher called a "frame of mind" and Bultmann an "understanding of existence," understanding of reality in which understandings of God, man, and world are all implicit, and in which no one has essential primacy over the other, nor indeed can any be sufficiently segregated from the others for such a debate to have ultimate substance. We have been in a period when modern theology and New Testament theology were cast primarily in terms of an understanding of existence. At the opening of this essay it was suggested that the new theology may well be cast primarily in terms of world, and the essay has concluded with the suggestion that New Testament theology could be so recast as well. The time may return when both can be cast primarily in terms of God. That would be neither the death nor the resurrection of theology, but simply another chapter in its history—or, as we might be inclined to put it today, theology in another "world."

VIII

JOHN CALVIN'S POLEMIC AGAINST IDOLATRY
John H. Leith

John Calvin's protest against idolatry is one of the dominating themes of his theology and churchmanship.[1] This protest is reflected in the very name "Reformed." In a general sense Lutheran and Calvinist are alike reformed, but the name was applied to the theological followers of Zwingli and Calvin because they were more radically reformed than the Lutherans.[2] One of the qualities that distinguished Calvinist theology from Lutheran theology, Alexander Schweizer observed more than a century ago, has been its emphasis upon the majesty of God and the dependence of all creatures upon him. While Lutheran theology was primarily concerned with Judaistic relapses into work-righteousness, Calvinism directed its strongest protest against paganism in the medieval church.[3]

Calvin does not contemplate the possibility of no-faith. Faith in the living God and idolatry exhaust the possibilities of human existence. The opening sentences of the *Institutes* describe man's situation in a very striking way.

> Nearly all the wisdom we possess, that is to say, true and sound wisdom, consists of two parts: the knowledge of God and of ourselves. But, while joined by many bonds, which one precedes and brings forth the other is not easy to discern. In the first place, no one can look upon himself without immediately turning his thoughts to the contemplation of God, in whom he "lives and moves" [Acts 17:28]. . . . Again, it is certain that man never achieves a clear knowledge of himself unless he has first looked upon God's face, and then descends from contemplating him to scrutinize himself.[4]

The very structure of existence forces man to deal with God and limits the possibilities of human existence to authentic faith and idolatry.[5] In the unified culture of Calvin's time these possibilities were for him almost exclusively expressed in the faith of a life reformed by the Word of God or in the idolatry of the Roman Church.[6] A pluralistic society today offers a greater variety of idolatries and perhaps more diversity in the forms of faith itself; but the basic options of existence, as Calvin understood it, remain the same. Man can either acknowledge God as God is or distort the divine reality.

I

Idolatry, Calvin contended, is man's effort to domesticate God and to conform him to man's definition of who He should be. It contradicts the fundamental rubric that "God himself is the sole and proper witness of himself."[7] God is not at man's disposal. He is the Creator of all things visible and invisible. He is the transcendent, free Lord. His authority and dignity are not to be confused with, shared with, or fastened to any created reality. God is sovereignly free in declaring who He is. Man can only listen, ceaselessly correcting and reforming his understanding of who God is.

Calvin knew, long before Feuerbach, that theology may be anthropology. He went so far as to write that "Man's mind, full as it is of pride and boldness, dares to imagine a god according to its own capacity; as it sluggishly plods, indeed is overwhelmed with the crassest ignorance, it conceives an unreality and an empty appearance as God."[8] While such a statement should not nullify Calvin's genuine appreciation for man's capacity to appropriate God's revelation in his creation as well as his special revelation in Jesus Christ, it underscores his awareness that man's hearing of the Word of God is always distorted by his own personal condition.

Every achievement of man in theology is limited on the one hand by man's finiteness and on the other hand by man's sin. God alone is the proper witness to himself. Man's witness is always broken, fragmented, and distorted. There are no infallible theologies and no infallible theologians. All theology is symbolic and fragmentary.

It can be argued that Calvin did not elaborate the methodology involved in this principle that God is his own proper witness. He could not have elaborated this principle for Scripture interpretation in the way that became necessary after the development of the tools of the historical method. He did not elaborate it for his own theology and ecclesiology. His theological concern was directed primarily to the violation of this principle in medieval and Roman Christianity; and for all his zeal for the principle, he left himself finally vulnerable at this point. He could never take seriously the fallibility of his own theology.[9]

Idolatry is more than the substitution of man's image of God for the God who is. It is also fastening God to some "thing." Calvin was well aware that men are too wise to believe that a piece of metal or stone, an emperor or a relic, is God. The problem is that God is tied to the finite and the determinate. In this way God is domesticated and controlled. Calvin puts this issue very clearly:

> For just as soon as a visible form has been fashioned for God, his power is also bound to it. Men are so stupid that they fasten God wherever they fashion him; and hence they cannot but adore. And there is no difference whether they simply worship an idol, or God in the idol. It is always idolatry when divine honors are bestowed upon an idol, under whatever pretext this is done. And because it does not please God to be worshiped superstitiously, whatever is conferred upon the idol is snatched away from Him.[10]

It must be carefully noted that idolatry is compatible with belief in God. Calvin never really contemplated the denial of God's existence, in any time a meaningless endeavor. Idolatry is the attempt to get control of God by objectifying his power and presence and fixing them in some "thing." Idolatry is the transference of something that belongs to God to some created reality.[11] It is the indiscriminate transference to the creature of what belongs to God alone.[12] In Calvin's judgment the pre-eminent example of this transference of the divine to created reality was the dignity accorded to angels and "saints" and the use of images in worship. The fact that "saints" and "angels" no longer figure in modern man's concern and that sculpture has been secularized must not be allowed to obscure the importance of the principle that Calvin is insisting upon. This principle is valid even though the application may vary. The principle is "that unless everything proper to his divinity resides in the one God, he is despoiled of his honor, and the reverencing of him profaned."[13] Idolatry is the objectification and domestication of God who is the free, creator Lord.

Idolatry is rooted in man's desire to domesticate and control God. This desire raises the further question, Why does man feel any need to acknowledge God in any way? The root of idolatry, Calvin said, is in man's nature, which is "a perpetual factory of idols."[14] Man is by nature religious. "There is within the human mind, and indeed by natural instinct, an awareness of divinity."[15] God implanted in every man a "sensus divinitatis" or a "semen religionis." This awareness of God is prior to critical reflection or interpretation of experience. It is immediate and existential. Hence religion is no arbitrary invention.[16] It is true that clever men have used religion for evil purposes, and religion may have been influenced by such experiences as fear. But religion would never have been so subject to perversion "if men's minds had not already been imbued with a firm conviction about God."[17] The history of religions is rooted in man's existential awareness of God and is, therefore, no accident or artificial contrivance.

The history of religion is not only rooted in man's awareness of the numinous but is also shaped by man's sin. Hence, the history of religions becomes for Calvin the history of idolatry. For idolatry itself is evidence of man's universal awareness of God.

> We know how man does not willingly humble himself so as to place other creatures over himself. Since, then, he prefers to worship wood and stone rather than to be thought of as having no God, clearly this is a most vivid impression of a divine being. So impossible is it to blot this from man's mind that natural disposition would be more easily altered, as altered indeed it is when man voluntarily sinks from his

natural haughtiness to the very depths in order to honor God![18]

II

The most obvious form of idolatry is the "worship" of the visible image of God. Imagery, whether painting or sculpture, violated Calvin's rubric that "God's glory is corrupted by an impious falsehood whenever any form is attached to him."[19] While Calvin believed that the Greeks who conceived God in human form were wiser than those who conceived him as sun, stars, or animal, he declares that God does not compare these images with one another for they are all inappropriate. Man's first errors concerning God did not begin with images, but these errors were quickly complicated by imagery.[20] When the Scriptures, which were written for the common man, want to distinguish the true God from the false, "it particularly contrasts him with idols," though this certainly does not mean that the more sophisticated speculations of the philosophers are any less serious deviations.[21]

Images had been used as the books of the uneducated. The medieval church had faced the herculean task of teaching the faith to barbarians who could neither read nor write, much less think abstractly. In retrospect, it may be said that Calvin did not fully appreciate this task. He admitted that not a few had to depend upon books in stone in his day, but this he attributed to the poor education they had received from those who trusted education to images. In short, he was convinced that images and art forms are ineffective ways of communicating the faith.

Calvin believed that the education that had divine warrant was by the preaching of the Word and the administration of the sacraments. "Paul testifies that by the true preaching of the gospel 'Christ is depicted before our eyes as crucified' [Gal. 3:1 b]. What purpose did it serve for so many crosses—of wood, stone, silver, and gold—to be erected here and there in churches, if this fact had been duly and faithfully taught: that Christ died on the cross . . . to reconcile us to God the Father [Rom. 5:10]? From this one fact they could have learned more than from a thousand crosses of wood or stone."[22]

Calvin had great confidence in the power of the written and spoken word. In his own style he worked for brevity, clarity, and reality.[23] He demanded correspondence between word and reality. He abhorred the empty, the artificial, and the contrived. He insisted that rhetoric must always serve communication, not ornamentation.[24] He himself achieved great skill in the use of the written and spoken word and became one of the most important creators of French as a medium for theological and philosophical discourse.[25] Perhaps Calvin's own skill tempted him to exaggerate the clarity of the written and spoken word and to fail to appreciate other forms of communication. There is, likewise, no question that he failed to reckon with the disparity between human words and reality.

Calvin's protest against images in worship and education leads to the question of his attitude toward the visual arts. The two issues must not be confused. Calvin is emphatic that sculpture and painting are gifts of God. He paid sculpture, painting, and music the tribute of taking them with great seriousness. He did not overlook what he considered their improper use, as one who was less aware of their power might have done. Calvin insisted in the first place upon the "pure and legitimate use" of art and painting.[26] One of his protests against images had been their inappropriate character. "The pictures or statues that they dedicate to saints—what are they but examples of the most abandoned lust and obscenity? If anyone wished to model himself after them, he would be fit for the lash. Indeed, brothels show harlots clad more virtuously and modestly than the churches show those objects which they wish to be thought images of virgins."[27]

Calvin insisted, secondly, that sculpture and painting should confine themselves to what was within man's reach. He protested against the pretension that sought to take heaven captive. "Only those things are to be sculptured or painted which the eyes are capable of seeing."[28] Calvin obviously had no appreciation for what is now called abstract art or for the power of art to communicate human emotions and commitments that cannot be visualized. This failure, however, does not touch the theological point that art must be realistic; that is, in conformity with reality.

He insisted upon this in literature, and he insisted upon it in art. Theologically, art is judged by its fidelity to the theological reality.

The visual arts that present histories and events can contribute to teaching. The representation of images and bodies without any depicting of past events can contribute to pleasure but, so far as Calvin could see, have nothing to contribute to teaching. The visual arts, therefore, play a very minor role in the communication of the faith. The visual arts were limited to representation of created reality. They also were ambiguous communicators in comparison with the clear and precise spoken and written word.

An assessment of Calvin's attitude toward the visual arts can point to his own limited achievement in appreciation of the arts. This is, however, to condemn Calvin for not being a universal man in the midst of a very busy life. A more significant assessment will judge him by his preference for verbal over against nonverbal forms of communication, a preference modified only by his doctrine of the sacraments and church music.

III

A second sharp focus of Calvin's polemic against idolatry is the Roman doctrine of the church and sacraments. This polemic has been summarized with remarkable insight by a Roman Catholic scholar.

> The Roman Catholicism he experienced convinced him that it was precisely the sovereignty of God which men had forgotten. To attribute to the church an exaggerated supernatural character, as though she herself were divinity, to endow the sacraments with an importance such that without them salvation was not possible and with them salvation thinkable only in reference to them, to encourage and abet the sacramental will-to-power of sacramental activity, to approve of rendering divinity to a thing in transubstantiation, to legislate the crassest theological materialism in which God is summoned by a formula and dismissed by digestion, to bind men's consciences with ritual posturings of human invention in which salvation is supposedly contained, and to prostitute service of God's glory to a benefice and to an assurance that the established disorder will continue in perpetuity, all of this was to sin against the sovereignty of God.

The sovereignty and divinity had not only been sinned against, but had been appropriated. And it was the goal of Calvin's theological endeavor to restore divinity to God.[29]

Calvin's protest against the divinization of the church comes to its climax in his judgment that the pope is the Antichrist. He is aware that this judgment seems to some slander and railing. Nevertheless, he maintains his position because "it is clear that the Roman pontiff has shamelessly transferred to himself what belonged to God alone and especially to Christ." The tyranny of the Roman pontiff is all the more serious because it "does not wipe out . . . the name of Christ or of the church but rather misuses a semblance of Christ and lurks under the name of the church as under a mask."[30]

This polemic of Calvin has appeared harsh and ruthless because of the very goodness of the pope. Hence Protestants have done penance by removing the offending passages from the creeds and theologies. This reaction is understandable enough, but it misunderstands the primary point that Calvin was making. Only that which is in some sense good can be the Antichrist. Hence a better penance would have been for Protestants to have applied this principle of historical judgment to their own church structures. Reinhold Niebuhr has made this point very clearly.

> The New Testament symbol of the Antichrist was appropriated by Catholicism primarily for the purpose of designating patent foes of the church. This polemic use of the symbol obscured the fact that the ultimate evil might not be the denial, but the corruption, of the ultimate truth. This is the point which the Protestant Reformation made in levelling the charge of Antichrist against the church itself. But neither Catholicism nor the Reformation used the symbol of the Antichrist effectively as a principle of general historical interpretation.[31]

Calvin emphasized the humanity of the church which lives by the forgiveness of sins.[32] The visible church that men can define must not be strictly identified with the church that is known to God. Hence, men must keep communion with the former but believe that the latter exists.[33] The church must be governed by councils because no man is good enough or wise enough to be trusted with absolute power. On the other hand, the councils must be composed of representatives because the mass of people is not wise or sober enough for the unlimited exercise of power.[34] In these ways Calvin underscored the humanity of the church and in theory balanced his high doctrine of the church and of the ministry as God's will for his people.

Calvin likewise protested against the divinization of the sacraments. This divinization came to sharp focus, so far as Calvin was concerned, in the doctrine of transubstantiation and in the sacrifice of the Mass. The doctrine of transubstantiation, as Calvin saw it, enabled men to master and control God. "They have forsaken the living God and fashioned a God after their own desire. For what is idolatry if not this: to worship the gifts in place of the Giver himself? In this there is a double transgression: for both the honor taken from God has been transferred to the creature (cf. Rom. 1:25), and he himself also has been dishonored in the defilement and profanation of his gift, when his holy Sacrament is made a hateful idol."[35]

> Now this perverse opinion, having been once accepted, has given rise to many other superstitions. And first, this carnal adoration, which is nothing but idolatry. For to prostrate oneself before the bread of the Supper, and to adore Jesus Christ in it as though he were there contained, is to make an idol displace the sacrament. We have no commandment to adore, but to take and eat.[36]

Calvin refused to "confine" the Word even in the Incarnation. "The Son of God descended from heaven in such a way that, without leaving heaven, he willed to be borne in the virgin's womb, to go about the earth, and to hang upon the cross; yet he continuously filled the world even as he had done from the beginning!"[37] In his study of the "extra Calvinisticum" David Willis writes: "Calvin is asserting that Christ is able to be God for us because he does not cease to be God over us in the Incarnation and because the humanity of Christ never ceases to be our humanity in the movement of God towards us."[38] Transubstantiation seemed to objectify and locate deity in a way that went beyond the Incarnation itself. This radical objectification of the divine into an impersonal "thing" that could be handled, carried about, and displayed did violence to Calvin's doctrine of God's transcendence and freedom. It also led to corrupting practices: reservation, processions, adoration of the Host, and the localization of the divine presence on the altar.

The sacrifice of the Mass likewise seemed to Calvin a presumptuous effort to control and use God. Luther, with his great protest against any form of work righteousness, had made the sacrifice of the Mass the focus of his complaint in the *Babylonian Captivity*. Calvin's main attention was directed to transubstantiation. Nevertheless, Calvin found much to say about the Mass as a means of controlling and using God. The difference between the sacrifice of the Mass and the Lord's Supper, Calvin declares, is the difference between giving and receiving. "Indeed, the Supper itself is a gift of God, which ought to have been received with thanksgiving. The sacrifice of the Mass is represented as paying a price to God, which he should receive by way of satisfaction."[39] In the sacrifice of the Mass, as Calvin sees it, man not only determines to deal with God on man's own terms, but man also substitutes priests for Christ, depriving Christ of his honor and snatching from him the prerogative of his eternal priesthood.[40]

John Calvin neither despaired of religion as the enemy of faith nor embraced it uncritically as man's authentic response to God's claim upon his life. He simply accepted religion as a universal fact, the inevitable destiny of men who have had implanted in them the "sensus divinitatis." He likewise accepted the structures, procedures, and rituals of the religious life as the proper instruments and forms of faith. The longest of the four books of the *Institutes,* "The External Means or Aids by Which God Invites Us Into the Society of Christ and Holds Us Therein," is devoted to the explication of the forms and structures of the life of faith. In part the motivation for Book Four is pragmatic. Men who live in time and space need effective ways of living the life of faith in this continuum. In part the motivation was theological. The structures and procedures may express faith or distort faith. They may in fact become surrogates for God or images to which God is fastened. For this reason, Calvin insists that all structures, procedures, and rituals are in themselves always reformable and finally dispensable. Only God's Word is essential. The church *is* when men hear and obey the divine Word. The church is God's elect. No historical structures can control or limit his grace.

IV

A third focus of Calvin's polemic against idolatry is the liturgy. In worship man is likewise tempted to domesticate and manipulate God, conforming God to man's own ideas of God, objectifying and localizing his presence and power in such a way as to use him. In commenting on the second commandment, Calvin writes, God "wholly calls us back and withdraws us from petty carnal observances, which our stupid minds, crassly conceiving of God, are wont to devise. And then he makes us conform to his lawful worship, that is, a spiritual worship established by himself. Moreover, he marks the grossest fault in this transgression, outward idolatry."[41] In idolatrous worship man transfers what belongs to God to the dead or to the saints;[42] or man, confident in his own ability, attempts "to wrest something from God by beating upon his ears with a garrulous flow of talk";[43] or man corrupts the service of God for the glorification or gain of man.[44] In all of Calvin's protest there is the recurring insistence that man must be open to the freedom and transcendence of God. Calvin's comment on the Lord's Prayer can be applied to worship in general.

> . . . in all prayer we ought carefully to observe that our intention is not to bind God to particular circumstances, or to prescribe at what time, in what place, or in what way he is to do anything. Accordingly, in this prayer we are taught not to make any law for him, or impose any condition upon him, but to leave to his decision to do what he is to do, in what way, at what time, and in what place it seems good to him. Therefore, before we make any prayer for ourselves, we pray that his will be done [Matt. 6:10]. By these words we subject our will to his in order that, restrained as by a bridle, it may not presume to control God but may make him the arbiter and director of all its entreaties.[45]

Calvin's concern about worship underscores its significance as the service of God and as a powerful determinant of personality and corporate life. Man is as he worships. Again, Calvin did not seriously consider the possibility that man would not worship. Out of natural feeling, necessity wrings some prayers from unbelievers just as much as from believers.[46] "God has planted in men's minds by nature the principle that their prayers are lawful only when their minds are uplifted. Hence the rite of lifting up the hands, . . . one common to all ages and peoples."[47] Hence, the real question is the how of worship. False worship may be more serious than false theology, though a false theology always expresses itself in a false worship. For this reason Calvin insisted that worship must be sincere, simple, intelligible, theologically sound, and open to the Word of God.

Worship that conforms to God's will for human life must be sincere. Calvin was always concerned for the real and opposed to all sham. He had no use for useless ceremonies and false externalities. Prayer is an "intimate conversation" with God, reverent and chaste.[48] Perfunctory, frivolous, and ostentatious prayers are an effrontery.[49]

Worship that conforms to God's will for human life must be simple. This is a recurring emphasis in Calvin's style in literature, in theology, in manner of life, and in worship. Pomp and show reflect man's pretense.[50] They are impressive and overpowering, but they are tricks that delude the eyes, that benumb rather than teach.[51] The Roman Catholic scholar Kilian McDonnell has written that Calvin saw in what he considered "ceremonial exhibitionism the theological cousin of Pelagianism."[52]

Worship that conforms to God's will for human life must also be intelligible. Prayers must be in the language of the people.[53] Music must be subordinate to understanding the words of the songs of worship.[54] The sacraments must be observed in the context of teaching.[55] The worshipers must understand what they are doing and why they are doing it. The theological intelligibility of worship provides the possibility of responsible decision and commitment. Calvin was determined, in a way unsurpassed in Christian history, to root out magic from religion; that is, the effort to control God by techniques that are independent of personal commitment.

Worship that conforms to God's will for human life must be

theologically sound. This is true not only of the administration of the sacraments but also of the prayers and of the singing. Calvin insisted, for example, that singing must be sound in music and in content. "We must add that singing not be frivolous and flighty— but poised and majestic, as St. Augustine says—and thus it is that there is a great difference between music that rejoices men at home while dining and the Psalms that are sung in Church and in the presence of God and his angels."[56]

The central fact in worship for Calvin was the proclamation of the Word of God. The whole liturgy was in fact the proclaiming of the Word that elicited man's response. Yet the sermon was sufficiently central in Calvin's actual practice that worship was sometimes called the preaching. Going to the sermon was synonymous with going to worship in Geneva. The decisive moment in the sacrament of the Lord's Supper is hearing and believing the words of the Institution. Baptism is administered only in the context of Christian proclamation and teaching.

Worship, as a human act, is never exempt from man's idolatrous proclivity. It is always in some measure the glorification of man. Prayer is always a mixture of faith and error.[57] The priority of the Word in worship is the corrective that constantly purifies worship. Calvin did not sufficiently emphasize that preaching itself has to be continually corrected, but the principle is implicit in his insistence on the priority of the Word in worship.

V

Calvin's theology was a mighty polemic against idolatry. In this he is our teacher. The idols of our time, to be sure, are not the idols of the sixteenth century. Yet the nature of man is still an idol factory. Men continue to substitute the figments of their imagination for God. We ought to know, much better than Calvin, that our gods are shaped by the way we make our living, by our wishes and dreams, and by the parochial pressures of our history. We know that God may only be the reification of our experience and that theology may be only anthropology. Indeed, we do know, as Calvin could not have known, that our theology always is in some real measure anthropology in both constructive and destructive ways.

No human achievement is ever final and absolute. Every achievement is limited by man's finiteness and waywardness. For this reason every word man speaks, every institution that he creates, and every society that he organizes must be criticized and reformed by the Word of God, spoken in Jesus Christ. This is the dynamism of Calvin. There is no stopping place, no resting place, no end of the journey. There is only the continual reformation of life by the Word of God in Jesus Christ. No man, no institution, no human achievement, ever hears or embodies this Word fully and completely. Therefore, the Calvinist is endlessly engaged in a warfare against idolatry in his own life, in the church, and in society.

This is a very difficult doctrine. For there is an inveterate tendency to lay hold of something that men have done and to fasten God to it. Men search for some resting place; but there is no resting place, only new summons to a new obedience. In W. H. Auden's "Christmas Oratorio," the shepherds rightly exclaim when they stand before the Christ child, "O here and now our endless journey starts."[58] This takes courage, the courage of true faith, that looks upon man's greatest achievement and demands reformation by the Christian community's apprehension of the Word of God in Jesus Christ.

IX

THEOLOGICAL PERSUASION
T. F. Torrance

Persuasion is the ability to win the agreement of those from whom we differ about something, but when we ask how this is done a distinction may be drawn. We may persuade people by convincing their minds and bringing them to assent to what we say, or we may persuade them by moving their feelings and evoking from them the response we desire. In both cases persuasion induces a belief and leads to a commitment, but in the former the controlling factor is a rational judgment rather than an emotive reaction. It is with the first that theological persuasion is principally concerned, but the second has a significant if subsidiary role to play in it as well. Persuasion of this kind would appear to presuppose that communication involves a triadic relation, that there is an inherent rationality in the nature of things, and that we are psychologically averse to change.

In normal acts of communication, in ordinary or scientific activity, we use language with a semantic intention; that is, not so much to express our minds as to refer other minds to something beyond ourselves. While our linguistic and conceptual forms may be communicated directly to other minds, intuitible realities are not directly communicable: we may point them out or refer to them through accepted signs or acquired designations in the hope that others will perceive or apprehend them also, but unless that takes place communication has not achieved its end. Communication takes place between minds that are directed to the same or similar objects and so is necessarily indirect through a triadic relationship, in which one mind directs another mind to an object by referring to it, and in which the other mind by following through the reference to the object understands the intention of the first mind.

This presupposes the rationality of the medium and the context in which communication takes place; that is, not only an intelligible language but an intelligible subject matter. The things about which we speak to one another must be capable of rational apprehension and of semantic designation. This is something that we assume and operate with in ordinary experience and in science, without attempting to explain it. If the nature of things were not somehow inherently rational they would remain inapprehensible and opaque, and indeed we ourselves would not be able to emerge into rationality. It is because things are amenable to rational treatment that we can apprehend them at all; we understand them or get light upon them insofar as we can penetrate into their rationality and develop our grasp of it. Scientific knowledge is that in which we bring the inherent rationality of things to light and expression, as we let the realities we investigate disclose themselves to us under our questioning and we on our part submit our minds to their inherent connections and order. Let it be granted that scientific activity involves a give-and-take between subject and object, and that all knowledge is by way of being a compromise between thought and being; nevertheless, it remains an awesome fact that if the nature of things were not inherently rational and apprehensible knowledge could not arise at all, far less communication. We communicate with other minds only when we can get them to submit their thought to the same rationality in things that we have experienced. Thus communication from the very start involves a persuasive element.

This basic persuasiveness is not one-directional, however, especially when we are engaged in a conjoint apprehension of things with other minds that communicate back to us, for in the fuller apprehension that we can have together of the same things there usually takes place a modification in our own apprehension of them and of their rationality. If something is inherently rational, and not merely accidental or surd-like, then it is our fault and not that of the thing itself if we fail to understand it: we have probably overlaid it with some form of unreality by bringing to its apprehension preconceived ideas that are not appropriate or are wrongly extrapolated from another field of experience. This means that as we seek to penetrate into the rationality of something our inquiry must also cut back into ourselves and into our own presuppositions, for they must be brought into question if we are to be really open to understand the thing concerned out of itself and in accordance with its own nature. In these circumstances persuasion must argue for a reconstruction in our interpretative frame of thought, in order that alien elements may be eliminated from it and new elements assimilated which are more appropriate to the nature of things we are speaking about.

This brings us to the other factor that we must presuppose in acts of communication and persuasion, that we are psychologically resistant to change in our habits of mind or modification in the structure of our thought, for it is we ourselves, the thinkers who live and work in those frames of thought, who have to be changed with them. Reason is and ought to be the slave of the passions, David Hume said rather outrageously, but in a sense very truly. Feeling is properly a passion, an affection in which we suffer impact or come under attack from something other than ourselves. We may resist it, and this makes it more difficult for us, but only if we go along with it (not necessarily to subscribe to it) may we know and understand it. This is the side of our rationality in which we let ourselves be affected by what we seek to know; we let it impose its own self-witness upon us, and we let ourselves be told by it (an all-important element in *a posteriori* knowledge). Doubtless this is where there arises a tension between pure science and a masterful technology, the tension between knowing a thing as we follow the clues it provides even when we have to "torment" it, as Francis Bacon expressed it, and the way of knowing in which we will accept only what we can make and shape according to our own stipulations. Obviously feeling enters into both ways of knowing, but since feeling arises we have to reckon with false feeling; that is, with feeling that has turned back upon itself, feeling that is more concerned to express itself and enjoy itself than to act appropriately to what is other than ourselves.

The situation is also complicated by the fact that no rational knowledge is merely *per modum causalitatis.* I cognize this table and typewriter truly when I let myself be compelled by what is there, and think accordingly. When I think thus under the compulsion of the facts I am rational, but I am irrational when I think that the table is a car and the typewriter is a steering wheel. Yet even though I think rationally as I am compelled to think in accordance with what is actually the case, I am free and not a puppet. There is a moment of the will here, in which I readily submit my mind to the compulsion of the nature of the facts upon me. Because there is this element of freedom, the moment of the will, where I am affected by what is there and where my feelings are roused, I must bring my feelings under disciplined control lest they be caught up in some movement or intention alien to the case in question at the moment.

But there is still another element that we have to take into account, the fact that in knowledge and communication, the reality to which we refer cannot be reduced to the forms of our thought and speech about it: being always breaks through the forms we use to apprehend it and will not be confined to them. Unless this were so we could not really know it, for then we could not distinguish what we know from our knowing of it. It is because knowledge involves this "relation of transcendent reference," as A. D. Ritchie has called it, that *judgment* plays a very important role in it, in relating the forms of thought and speech to the reality concerned and in judging their adequacy in the light of it, and thus in developing the appropriate mode of knowing and the apposite mode of speaking about it. This is a difficult element in the act of communication, because there is inevitably a discrepancy between the signitive forms we use and the realities themselves. Hence if communication is to succeed we have to refer to some reality in such a way that we will lead others to form the right judgment in regard to it, for without that they cannot know it or speak about it aright.

In persuasion we are not concerned with "an artful manipulation of language," in John Stuart Mill's sense, but with getting another to submit his mind to the facts and to think of them in accordance with their nature; yet in order to do that we must often use a persuasive form of words, and that is a real art. Because art is involved, persuasion may lapse into sophistry or mere rhetoric. Ultimately we persuade a person of something by convincing him that it is the case; that is, by appealing to its truth or by deceiving him into thinking that what we say of it is true. In persuasion we seek to direct the mind of another to something in such a way that it falls under the compulsion of its reality, and cannot but assent to it. But since we never know merely *per modum causalitatis,* and cannot communicate what we know directly, the elements of feeling, will, freedom, and judgment enter in, and we have to learn how to cope with them faithfully. To persuade someone about something we may have to dig his mind out of a bigoted obsession with a false framework, or seek to wean it from misdirected feeling and heal it of false motivation. Hence in, persuasion we have to be able to *move* people and to *convince* them at the same time: that is, to jolt them out of the situation in which their own unrealities and artificialities obscure the truth from them, and to direct them to the reality concerned in such a way that they really see it as it is and as it shows itself out of its own inherent rationality. To *convince* a person of the truth must remain primary and dominant in persuasion, but to move him to adopt the right attitude where a rational judgment can be made in the light of the truth will play a significant if subsidiary role. Whenever we seek to move people through their feelings without leading them to submit their minds to the compulsion of the actual facts, persuasion has lapsed from its integrity; and whenever we abstract language and argument from their proper semantic function and use them in their detachment emotively to evoke the desired reactions or artfully to contrive the acceptance of certain ideas, persuasion has given way to sophistry.

All this applies to theological persuasion as much as to authentic persuasive activity in any other field of experience or knowledge, but in theology there are special factors that have to be taken into account. That is as it should be, for in every field of experience, as John MacMurray has shown us so clearly, we behave rationally when we act in accordance with the nature of an object, and allow it to prescribe to us the specific mode of rationality we have to adopt toward it as well as the kind of demonstration appropriate to it. Thus when we take into account the difference in the nature of the object of theological knowledge we discern the difference between "discovery" and "revelation." In natural science, discovery is the heuristic activity in which we seek to advance beyond what we know to what is radically new and which we can learn only out of itself. We speak here about "interrogating" some reality in order to let it "reveal itself" or "declare itself" to us, but actually that reality is mute or dumb, for we have not only to frame our own questions to it but to frame its answers to us. In theological knowledge, however, we do not have to do with a mute or dumb reality (that would be an idol) but with One who acts upon us and addresses us in his Word, where the expressions "reveal itself" and "declare itself" are really in place. Here we discover what is new through giving our ear to it, and by letting ourselves be told what we could never tell ourselves. This is what is meant by divine revelation. However, both discovery and revelation have to be put to the test to see whether they really are what is claimed; i.e., to see whether it is really discovery or simply a pure invention, and to see whether it is really revelation or merely imagination on our part. At the same time we have to test the referential relations of our statements to make sure that they are relevant to the realities to which they refer. Here, then, we have a basic common factor, and yet, in accordance with the difference in the nature of each kind of reality, a difference between the mode of knowledge that is a form of discovery and the mode of knowledge that is grounded in divine revelation.

This difference affects our acts of communication and persuasion, for here it is God in his Word who forms with us the triadic relation: he takes an active part in our communicating and persuading. We may express this in another way by saying that we are concerned here with a *different kind of rationality* from that which we find embedded in nature—in the geometrical patterns of crystals or the periodicity of the elements, for example. What we discover there is amenable to mathematical treatment and formulation, the kind of rationality which we call "number," but we cannot think in this way of divine acts which we may apprehend only in accordance with their divine rationality which we call "Logos" or "Word." Confusion between these two would be the equivalent of a "category-mistake" of a very grave order. If therefore we are to communicate with someone about God and to persuade him in respect of something about God we must refer him to the divine Logos in order that he may listen to God for himself, for he cannot know God unless he lets God bear witness to himself and disclose himself through his own Word.

In theological persuasion we seek to bring others to the point where they submit their minds to the inherent rationality of the divine revelation. There they must think only as they are compelled to think by the nature of the divine realities themselves, and there they must engage in a critical judgment in which they test the persuasive statements in the light of that to which they refer, and test their own preconceptions to see whether they are importing into what is apprehended something that is not really there or whether they are preventing the apprehension of what is really there but is quite new and altogether beyond them. This kind of persuasion cannot achieve its end fully with single individuals, for if God is not merely what I have thought up and projected out there, he is objectively real and universally knowable by others (that is, insofar as they are prepared to know him in accordance with his own nature). If this is so, my knowing of God will involve not only a private conscience (*con-scientia*) between myself and God, but a conscience which I share with others knowing him and in which I submit my private conscience to critical testing in the light of that of others. This will then become part of the test of whether it is really God I know or an invention of my own.

In natural science we build up knowledge through casting ourselves upon the rationality of the given, and we test the reality and objectivity of our knowledge through the development of its inherent patterns of rationality in a way that not only transcends our experience in the present but proves to be progressively fertile in the light it throws upon other problems and questions. But this testing requires a whole community of verifiers all over the world, for science moves and advances as one, with its

internal self-scrutiny and self-criticism, and its own rigorous conscience aroused in it by the compelling claims of reality. So it is
with theology. We cannot know God one by one in isolation, for
we require the objectivity of one another to help us escape
from our own inturned subjectivities. We learn to know God
conjointly and by being assimilated to a community of conscience,
ranging across the ages as well as the world, in which our critical
judgments are intertwined and we are subjected to critical questioning and correcting from one another. It is in such a community
and continuity of interpretation and understanding that communication takes place, and from it that we seek to persuade others
to believe—that is, to induce in others the rational assent which
in good conscience we believe they must give if they let their
thinking fall under the compelling rationality of the divine Word.

What steps in fact do we normally take in efforts at theological
persuasion?

The first and most prevalent, though doubtless the most misused, is *proclamation,* which is not meant to be "preaching at"
people but to refer them away from themselves to divine and
transcendent realities. It is essentially a kerygmatic, ostensive act
in which we point out what God has done and bear witness to his
self-revelation, with the intention of focusing people's attention
upon God himself, and of bringing them within "hearing distance"
of his Word that they may hear and believe for themselves.
Proclamation that is faithful to the way in which God meets us
in his Word calls for a corresponding mode of apprehension, the
response of faith in which, as Luther put it, we have to "stick
our eyes in our ears."

Along with this, however, theological persuasion supplies didactic
material; that is, some unfolding of the conceptual content of the
divine Word which will provide hearers with an *interpretative
framework* to guide their recognition and give their minds some
hold upon what they apprehend. It enables them to penetrate
into the inherent rationality of the Word so that they may form
their own judgments and yield their rational assent as their minds
come under the power of its inner logic. It cannot be understood
or appropriated from an alien framework, but requires one that

has been developed on the same ground on which knowledge of God has actually arisen and which is therefore appropriate to it. To cite St. Thomas, *Deus non est in genere*—he may be understood only out of himself and through the conceptual content of his own Word, since he is not in a class with others.

These two operations have to be taken together and held together at two logical levels, for one acts as meta-language to the other, and neither can be worked into a complete or consistent system without the other. This is what we have learned in other fields from Frege and Gödel. We cannot explain clearly what $2 \times 2 = 4$ means without using word-language and moving on to a different logical level with its wider syntactical system. Hence from the point of view of logical form, the parables of Jesus and his own reported interpretations belong integrally together, for the parabolic language of faith-knowledge requires integration with the wider syntactical formalization provided by the interpretative framework found already in the Gospels, and indeed apart from the conceptual content of that framework the parables are not really applicable to existence.

Now we come to the real difficulties with which theological persuasion has to cope, the fact that in theological knowledge we are up against a *new way* of thinking, with its own new conceptions and its apposite, if strange, formalization. The assimilation of what is radically new always involves an arduous struggle, for we are afraid of breaking logical form and accepting what from the perspective of prior form inevitably appears a-logical or may even appear absurd. No one has written more helpfully than Michael Polanyi about this problem as it is found within natural science when a new framework arises segregated from any knowledge or alleged knowledge rooted in different conceptions of experience. We may cite him at length.

> The two conflicting systems of thought are separated by a logical gap, in the same sense as a problem is separated from the discovery which solves the problem. Formal operations relying on *one* framework of interpretation cannot demonstrate a proposition to persons who rely on *another* framework. Its advocates may not even succeed in getting a

hearing from these, since they must first teach them a new language, and no one can learn a new language unless he first trusts that it means something. . . . Proponents of a new system can convince their audience only by first winning their intellectual sympathy for a doctrine they have not yet grasped. Those who listen sympathetically will discover for themselves what they would otherwise never have understood. Such an acceptance is a heuristic process, a self-modifying act, and to this extent a conversion. It produces disciples forming a school, the members of which are separated for the time being by a logical gap from those outside it.

And again, from the same page:

We can now see . . . the great difficulty that may arise in the attempt to persuade others to accept a new idea in science. We have seen that to the extent to which it represents a new way of reasoning, we cannot convince others of it by formal argument, for so long as we argue within their framework, we can never induce them to abandon it. Demonstration must be supplemented, therefore, by forms of persuasion which can induce a conversion. The refusal to enter on the opponent's way of arguing must be justified by making it appear altogether unreasonable.[1]

The fact that Polanyi has had recourse, to some extent at any rate, to the language of the New Testament, to help him express the difficult process of apprehending and assimilating a new scientific conception is an indication that we do have common factors between scientific and theological persuasion. But what are the supplementary ways of persuasion that theology must use? These are *worship* and *evangelism*. Worship is the exercise of the mind in the contemplation of God in which wonder and awe play an important part in stretching and enlarging our vision, or in opening up our conceptual forms to take in that which by its nature far outruns them. That is why worship goes together with the kerygmatic activity in proclamation whereby we are directed by ostensive acts of reference far beyond ourselves to "the mighty acts of God." Polanyi himself speaks of worship as "heuristic vision,"[2] but it is the same thing, *mutatis mutandis,* that C. F. von Weizäcker speaks of in science as *meditation* in which we make a transition to a different level of thinking. He describes meditation as "the process by which consciousness takes possession of a truth in such a way that not only the content but also the structure of consciousness is changed."[3]

We may reconstruct this by saying that worship is meditation in which we are engaged in heuristic audition, in which we make a transition from the observable to what cannot be observed but may be heard, and from the world of created realities to the Creator himself. To "see God" we must renounce the criterion of perceptibility and learn to "hear" him, but hear him in a mode corresponding to the nature of his Word. It is worship that gives our conceptual forms the open texture they require in theological knowledge, and it is prayer that gives our interrogation of divine realities the appropriate mode of "discovery" in which we do not force God's self-disclosure to conform to our stipulations but find ourselves profoundly questioned before him. Apart from the "relation of transcendent reference" which we acquire in worship, everything goes wrong epistemologically; prayer becomes a sort of frustrated soliloquy, and knowledge of God is redacted to a form of objectified self-understanding. And we do not even get off the ground, as it were.

But what about *evangelism,* for this too is essential? This is where theological persuasion hurts us, not simply because we are psychologically averse to change and not simply because our prior knowledge and our self-understanding which it enshrines have to be reconstructed to take in the new elements, but because we who stand behind our questioning and who exist in our frameworks of thought are *hostile to the truth of God and require to be reconciled to it.* In every field of knowledge and communication we have to have sympathy with the subject matter concerned, although this is much more important in the human sciences and especially in psychology; but in the field of theological knowledge above all, we have to reckon with the stubborn fact of our deeply ingrained self-centeredness and selfishness which must be torn wide open if we are to know God in accordance with his nature— that is, in *love.* This is why theological persuasion must be evangelistic, for it must show to people that they exist in enmity to the ways of God and require to "repent and be converted" if they are to know the truth. Let it be granted that evangelism is only too often misused, as it is certainly abused by many, but at its heart evangelism is simply the attempt to *persuade*. It announces the fact that God was in Christ reconciling the world to himself, and does not impute to us our sins but freely offers us forgiveness and love. And so, as St. Paul expressed it, "We are ambassadors for Christ, as though God did beseech you by us: we pray you in Christ's stead, be ye reconciled to God."[4] In the passage cited, this is set within an interpretative framework that explains what is involved and seeks to bring the mind of the reader directly under the constraint of the love of Christ—that is, the logic of God as he has translated it into our human existence. Evangelists are not so far wrong when they insist that if we do not believe it is not because we cannot but because we do not want to, for our self-centeredness is resistant to the claims of the divine love; but they are wrong if they play rhetorical tricks upon people's fears and anxieties and work up their feelings in order to move them to believe. Yet this is certain, that theological persuasion cannot succeed without the subsidiary work of moving people to renounce themselves and leave their inappropriate ways of thinking, although its primary work is to induce *rational conviction* and belief in the light of the overwhelming Truth of God as it is in Jesus Christ.

WILLIAM CHILDS ROBINSON

FAMILY: Born, Lincolnton, North Carolina, December 4, 1897. Parents, David W. and Edith Childs Robinson. Reared in Columbia, South Carolina. Married Mary McConkey, June 22, 1921. Children, William C., Jr., born 1922 and James McC., born 1924.

EDUCATION: A.B., Roanoke College; M.A., University of South Carolina; B.D., Columbia Theological Seminary; Th.M., Princeton Theological Seminary; Th.D., Harvard University; D.D., Roanoke College; Graduate Study at Basel, Cambridge, and Rome.

CHURCHES: Pastor, Gettysburg Presbyterian Church, 1921-26; Supply Pastor, Covington, Georgia; First Presbyterian Church, Charlotte, N. C.; Reid Memorial, Augusta; West End, Pryor Street, Morningside, Westminster, Capitol View, Atlanta.

Moderator, Presbytery of Carlisle; Presbytery of North Alabama; Synod of Alabama; Member General Council, Assembly's Committee on Research; Delegate to World Council.

LECTURES: Free Church Lectures, Edinburgh, 1938
James Sprunt Lectures, Richmond, 1941
Payton Lectures, Fuller, 1949
Alumni Lectures, Columbia, 1961
R. L. Robinson Lectures, Erskine, 1967
Several courses at Candler School of Theology, Emory University

PUBLICATIONS:

A. Books

Columbia Theological Seminary and the Southern Presbyterian Church, 1831-1931 (Lindsay Printing Co., Decatur, 1931), based on Doctoral Dissertation presented at Harvard University, 1928.

The Certainties of the Gospel, Zondervan, 1935.

What Is Christian Faith?, Zondervan, 1937.

The Word of the Cross, Free Church Lectures, Edinburgh, 1938, London, S.G.U. translated and published in Korean by Christian Book Association.

Our Lord, An Affirmation of the Deity of Christ, 1937, 2nd edition 1949, Eerdmans.

Christ, the Hope of Glory, The James Sprunt Lectures 1941, Eerdmans, 1945.

Christ, the Bread of Life, The Payton Lectures, Eerdmans, 1950.

The Reformation: A Rediscovery of Grace, the Columbia Alumni Lectures, Eerdmans, 1962.

Repeated as the R. L. Robinson Lectures at Erskine Theological Seminary, 1967.

Editor and writer of opening chapter of *Who Say Ye That I Am?,* Eerdmans, 1949.

Translator with J. M. Robinson of Eduard Thurneysen, *The Sermon on the Mount,* John Knox Press, 1964, and S.P.C.K.

Promoted and wrote Introduction to R. R. MacGregor's translation of Pierre C. Marcel, *The Relevance of Preaching,* Baker, 1963.

B. Booklets, Articles, Bulletins

"The Holy Spirit in the Holy Scriptures," Committee on Woman's Work, Atlanta, 1935.

"An Interview with Professor Karl Barth," Bulletin C.T.S., 1938.

"The Theocentric Theology Implicit in the Name of

the Trinity," *The Evangelical Quarterly* and Bulletin C.T.S., 1934.

"The Theology of Jesus and the Theology of Paul," *The Evangelical Quarterly* and Bulletin C.T.S., 1937.

"The Bodily Resurrection of Jesus Christ," *Theologische Zeitschrift,* Basel, April 1957, and Bulletin C.T.S.

"Understanding the Church," Executive Committee of Christian Education and Publication, Richmond, 1948.

"God's Hand over Man's," Charlotte, N. C. (The Mystery of Providence), 1941.

"The Christian Faith according to the Shorter Catechism," Weaverville, 1950.

"Architecture Appropriate to Reformed Worship," Weaverville, 1956.

"God and the State, a Plea for Prayer in the Schools," Bulletin C.T.S., 1964.

"A Re-study of the Virgin Birth," *The Evangelical Quarterly,* December 1965.

"What Think Ye of Christ?" A Study in the Christology of the RSV, Weaverville, 1953.

"Affirmations of the Atonement in Current Theology," *Christianity Today,* March 1967. Address to Bible Conference, Montreat, N. C.

" 'Abba' The Christ Child's Word for God," *Christianity Today,* May 13, 1966. Lecture to Society of Biblical Literature, Southern Section.

"The Inspiration of Scripture," accepted for publication in *Christianity Today,* Spring 1968. Address to Ministers' Institute, Montreat, N. C., 1966.

"The Headship of Christ," *Christianity Today,* April 29, 1957.

"God Incarnate for Suffering Men," Easter sermon at Warm Springs, April 1, 1945, the last sermon heard by President Franklin D. Roosevelt. Printed by S.P.J., Weaverville, 1945.

"The Faith of a Soldier," Weaverville, 1942.

"The Prayer of a Soldier," Weaverville, 1944.

"Soldier, Sailor, Sparrow: Not One Shall Fall without Your Father," Weaverville, 1943.

C. Contributions to Symposiums, et al.

"Predestination" in *Basic Christian Doctrines,* ed. by C. F. H. Henry, N. Y., 1962.

"The Tolerance and the Intolerance of Calvin" in *J. Calvin, Contemporary Prophet,* ed. by J. T. Hoogstra, Baker, 1959.

"The Nature of the Church" in *Christian Faith and Modern Theology,* ed. by C. F. H. Henry, N. Y., 1964.

"Evolution, Is the Mirage Lifting?" in *Science and Religion,* ed. by J. C. Monsma, Putnam, 1962.

"Church, Lord, Lamb of God, Reconciliation, Wrath" in Baker's *Dictionary of Theology.*

"Auferstehung im N. T." in *Biblisch-Historisches Handwörterbuch,* ed. by B. Reicke and Leonard Rost and reprinted as

"The Resurrection" in *Interpretation,* April, 1962.

"Kristoui Yuksinjok Puwhal," *Sinhak Chinam,* 1958 (Seoul: Presbyterian Theological Seminary), pp. 56-71.

Sipjaka wa Kidokkyo (Seoul: Christian Literature Society of Korea, n.d.), 156 pp.

NOTES AND ACKNOWLEDGMENTS

II. JESUS IS LORD

F. F. Bruce

1. Werner Kramer, *Christ, Lord, Son of God* (London: SCM Press Ltd., 1966), pp. 67-71.

2. We need not here discuss the proposed emendation to χριστὸς κυρίου (as in Ps. Sol. 17:36).

3. By F. Hahn, *Christologische Hoheitstitel* (Göttingen, 1966), pp. 95 ff.

4. J. A. T. Robinson, "The Most Primitive Christology of All?" in *Twelve New Testament Studies* (London, 1962), pp. 139 ff.

5. O. Bauernfeind, *Die Apostelgeschichte* (Leipzig, 1939), pp. 66 ff.

6. A. M. Ramsey, 'What Was the Ascension?' *S. N. T. S. Bulletin* 2 (1952), pp. 43 ff., especially p. 49; E. Schweizer, *Lordship and Discipleship* (London, 1960), pp. 74 f.

7. Adolf Deissmann, *Light from the Ancient East* (New York: George H. Doran Company, 1927), pp. 353-354.

8. Dio Cassius, *Hist.* lxii. 5.2.

9. Suetonius, *Domitian* 13.2.

10. *Mart. Polyc.* 8:2.

11. See on this F. Hahn, *Christologische Hoheitstitel,* pp. 68 f.

12. *Didache* 10:6.

13. H. Lietzmann, *Messe und Herrenmahl* (Bonn, 1926), p. 210.

14. Cf. the explanations given by W. Bousset in *Kyrios Christos* (Göttingen, ¹1913), p. 103, (²1921), p. 84, and in *Jesus der Herr* (Göttingen, 1916), pp. 22 f., and by Rudolf Bultmann in *Theology of the New Testament,* I (London, 1952), p. 52.

15. The various forms of early LXX representation of YHWH and the question whether synagogue usage lay behind any of them cannot be discussed here. In the Peshitta both YHWH and *'ādōn* are rendered here by *mar* (*māryā* and *mārī* respectively). The later "official" Targums make David himself the person addressed by YHWH; in *Midrash Tehillim* the person addressed is Abraham.

16. It is a pleasure to mention the most recent monograph on Philippians 2:5-11, by my colleague R. P. Martin: *Carmen Christi* (Cambridge, 1967).

III. PAUL'S UNDERSTANDING OF RIGHTEOUSNESS

Bo Reicke

1. J. Gonda, *Deiknymi* (1929), pp. 224-232; H. Kleinknecht & G. Schrenk, δίκη in *Theol. Wörterb.*, 2 (1935), pp. 180-183; H. Rosmann, "Justificare" in *Verbum Domini* 21 (1941), pp. 144-147; D. Loenen, *Dike* (1948), pp. 1-13, 87-95; Hj. Frisk, *Griechisches etymologisches Wörterbuch*, 1 (1960), pp. 355 f., 393 f.

2. In the modern discussion, traditional positions are sometimes exchanged, as is found in two interesting studies both inspired by a paper of R. Bultmann's disciple E. Käsemann. (1) The Protestant author P. Stuhlmacher refers God's righteousness to creation and salvation history (what he prefers to call *Wortgeschehen*), and says justification is no mere imputation, but a real making righteous: *Gerechtigkeit Gottes bei Paulus* (1965), pp. 175, 220, 236. In spite of his attack on synergism, p. 220, this implies appreciation of Catholic traditions. (2) Preferably quoting Protestant authorities, the Catholic scholar K. Kertelge supports a forensic and eschatological interpretation of justification: *"Rechtfertigung" bei Paulus* (1967), pp. 68 f., 72, 112-160. He agrees with Käsemann and Stuhlmacher in many respects, and is also inclined to believe that Paul took over his fundamental conceptions from Jewish apocalypticism, p. 308. But he deplores the fact that Stuhlmacher leaves the basis Bultmann has laid by his anthropological perspective, p. 309.

3. The kingship of God was referred to in connection with righteousness by G. Quell, δίκη in *Theol. Wörterb.* 2 (1935), pp. 178 f.; and G. Schrenk, *ibid.*, pp. 200, 206-208. Schrenk also saw the error of regarding the juridical and mystical aspects of righteousness as two different "craters" of Paul's so-called doctrine: *ibid.*, p. 212. A reference to Christ's lordship would have made their unity even more evident.

IV. PAUL AND THE LAW

George Eldon Ladd

1. See Walther Eichrodt, *Theology of the Old Testament* (London: SCM Press, Ltd., 1961), I, ch. II; G. A. F. Knight, *Law and Grace* (London: SCM Press, Ltd., 1962), pp. 25-26.

2. H. Kleinknecht, *Bible Key Words: Law* (New York: Harper & Row, 1962), p. 27. "The Law of Moses in itself was originally given not as a code the observance of which was necessary to salvation, but as a set of principles for the guidance of the people of God." (R. McL. Wilson, "Nomos," *StTh*, 5 [1952], p. 39.)

3. The primary concept of "life" in the Old Testament is not the life of the age to come, as in Daniel 12:2, but the enjoyment of the good gifts of God in fellowship with God in this life.

4. Gerhard von Rad, in *Theological Dictionary of the New Testament*, ed. by Gerhard Kittel (Grand Rapids: Wm. B. Eerdmans Publishing Co., 1964), II, p. 845. See also his essay on "Law" in *Old Testament Theology* (Edinburgh: Oliver and Boyd, 1965), II, pp. 388-409, where he shows that the apostasy of Israel consisted not in breaking individual commandments, but in failing to respond to God's saving acts for his people.

5. See John Bright, *The Kingdom of God* (New York: Abingdon Press, 1953), p. 94.

6. For other references, see Kleinknecht, *op. cit.,* p. 76; Strack and Billerbeck, *Kommentar* III, pp. 129 ff., 237. Schoeps recognizes the change in the concept of the law in apocryphal writings and the LXX, but not in classical Judaism. He maintains that Paul's opposition to the law was based in part upon this distortion and misrepresentation of the law in Hellenistic Judaism. (H. J. Schoeps, *Paul* [London: Lutterworth Press, 1961], pp. 215-218.)

7. See such writings as *The Testaments of the Twelve Patriarchs, The Hymns of the Qumran Community*. See Richard N. Longenecker, *Paul Apostle of Liberty* (New York: Harper & Row, 1964), chapter III. Longenecker differentiates between "legalism" with its emphasis on law-keeping as a human action, and "nomism" which offers obedience to the law as the reaction to the goodness and saving acts of God—an expression of trust in God.

8. Emil Schürer, *A History of the Jewish People in the Time of Jesus Christ* (New York: Charles Scribner's Sons, 1890), II, ii, pp. 77, 84, 115-117; George Foot Moore, *Judaism in the First Centuries of the Christian Era* (Cambridge: Harvard University Press, 1927), I, p. 291.

9. Moore, *op. cit.,* I, p. 465.

10. See Schoeps, *op. cit.,* pp. 177, 193.

11. Joseph Bonsirven, *Palestinian Judaism in the Time of Jesus Christ* (New York: Holt, Rinehart and Winston, Inc., 1964), p. 95.

12. See Moore, *op. cit.,* I, pp. 467-469. We are dependent on Moore for the summary that follows.

13. *Ibid.,* I, p. 494.

14. *Ibid.,* I, pp. 266, 526.

15. *Ibid.,* I, pp. 114, 117, 500.

16. *Ibid.,* I, pp. 520-521.

17. *Ibid.,* I, pp. 532-533.

18. *Ibid.,* I, pp. 500-504, 508.

19. Schoeps, *op. cit.,* p. 196.

20. *Ibid.,* p. 213.

21. *Ibid.,* p. 216, quoting Mekhilta Ex. 20:6.

22. See J. Behm in *TDNT*, II, pp. 128-129.

23. See Moore, *op. cit.,* II, pp. 16-21.

24. "All Israelites have a share in the world to come." See Herbert Danby, *The Mishnah* (London: Oxford University Press, 1933), p. 397.

25. Schoeps, *op. cit.*, p. 196.

26. Moore, *op. cit.*, II, p. 387.

27. *Ibid.*, II, p. 318. The text from *Tosefta Sanhedrin*, xiii, 3 ff., is quoted by J. Bonsirven, *op. cit.*, pp. 250-251.

28. Enoch 47:3; 81:4; 89:61-70; 90:20; 98:7-8; 104:7; Apoc. Bar. 24:1; IV Ez. 6:20; Asc. Isa. 9:22; Jub. 30:22; Aboth 3:17.

29. IV Ez. 7:77; 8:33; Apoc. Bar. 14:12; Ps. Sol. 9:9.

30. Test. Abr. 13; En. 41:1; 61:8; Ps. Sol. 5:6; Pesikta 26. See J. Bonsirven, *op. cit.*, p. 239; Fr. Weber, *Jüdische Theologie* (1897), pp. 379 ff.

31. W. Gutbrod, *BKW: Law* (1962), p. 119.

32. See C. H. Dodd, *The Meaning of Paul for Today* (London: The Swarthmore Press Ltd., 1920), pp. 71-73. Others who follow this autobiographical interpretation of Romans 7 are Adolf Deissmann, *St. Paul* (London: Hodder and Stoughton, 1926), pp. 92-98; W. D. Davies, *Paul and Rabbinic Judaism* (S.P.C.K., 1948), pp. 24-27; Joseph Klausner, *From Jesus to Paul* (London: Allen & Unwin, Ltd., 1944), pp. 497-499; A. C. Purdy, *IDB*, III, pp. 685, 692. John Murray, *The Epistle to the Romans* (Grand Rapids, Mich.: Wm. B. Eerdmans Publishing Co., 1959), I, p. 255, sees an unregenerate man under conviction of sin. John Knox, "Romans," *The Interpreter's Bible*, IX, p. 499, thinks Paul describes both past and present experience.

33. On the theological significance of boasting, see Rudolf Bultmann, *TDNT*, III, p. 649; *Theology of the New Testament* (New York: Charles Scribner's Sons, 1951), I, p. 242.

34. See C. G. Montefiore, *Judaism and St. Paul* (1914), p. 93; Samuel Sandmel, *A Jewish Understanding of the New Testament* (Cincinnati: Hebrew Union College Press, 1956), pp. 37-51; H. J. Schoeps, *op. cit.*, pp. 198, 206, 218.

35. G. F. Moore, *op. cit.*, I, 271-272. See also W. D. Davies, *Torah in the Messianic Age and/or the Age to Come* (Philadelphia: Society of Biblical Literature, 1952), who cites some evidence for the expectation of a modified Torah in the messianic age. Schoeps cites rabbinic sayings which anticipated the cessation of the law in the messianic kingdom as a basis for Paul's view of the abolition of the law (*op. cit.*, pp. 171-172). However, this is not the prevailing Jewish view, and Paul does not teach the complete *abolition* of the law. See also Longenecker, *op. cit.*, pp. 128-132.

36. See G. Schrenk in *TDNT*, I, 765 ff.

37. Roy A. Harrisville, *The Concept of Newness in the New Testament* (Minneapolis: Augsburg Publishing House, 1960), 60. It is recognized by W. D. Davies, *op. cit.*, p. 225. Davies points out that this emphasis is largely missing in rabbinic Judaism.

38. Longenecker, *op. cit.*, pp. 144-147.

39. See below, p. 29, for the permanence of the law.

40. See Longenecker (*op. cit.*, pp. 245-252), who comes to similar conclusions from the perspective of Paul's doctrine of liberty.

41. W. Gutbrod, *BKW: Law,* p. 46.

42. Romans 3:10-18 cites passages from Isaiah and Psalms as utterances of the *nomos* (3:19). First Corinthians 14:21 quotes Isaiah 28:11 as *nomos.*

43. See C. H. Dodd, "The Law," in *The Bible and the Greeks* (London: Hodder & Stoughton, 1935), pp. 25-41.

44. C. K. Barrett, *A Commentary on the Epistle to the Romans* (New York: Harper & Brothers, 1957), p. 44.

45. *Ibid.,* pp. 56 ff. See for a similar interpretation Leonhard Goppelt, *Jesus, Paul and Judaism* (Camden, N. J.: Thomas Nelson & Sons, 1964), p. 137.

46. See above, p. 8.

47. See Moore, *op. cit.,* III, pp. 150-151.

48. Barrett, *op. cit.,* p. 58.

49. Moore, *op. cit.,* I, p. 491.

50. See J. Behm, *TDNT,* II, p. 129.

51. J. Schniewind, *TDNT,* II, p. 582.

52. H. J. Schoeps, *op. cit.,* pp. 174, 183. However, this reinterpretation is due to his Christian perspective and not to the Hellenistic background which Schoeps assumes.

53. These verses describe a time of immaturity and subjection in contrast to maturity and freedom. *Eis Christon* (vs. 24) should therefore be rendered "until Christ" (RSV), not "to bring us unto Christ" (KJV).

54. See Goppelt, *op. cit.,* p. 147. Also Moore, *op. cit.,* III, p. 151.

55. See above, pp. 11-12, for this interpretation.

56. See William Sanday and Arthur C. Headlam, *Romans* (Edinburgh: T. & T. Clark, 1895), pp. 184-186; W. David Stacey, *The Pauline View of Man* (London: Macmillan & Co., Ltd., 1956), p. 212. C. L. Mitton, "Romans VII Reconsidered," *ET,* 65 (1953/4), pp. 78 ff., 99 ff., 132 ff., considers it to be the Christian who falls back into reliance on the law; F. F. Bruce, *The Epistle of Paul to the Romans* (London: The Tyndale Press, 1963), pp. 150-151, the Christian who lives in two ages at once.

57. This viewpoint was supported by Jas. Denney, *Romans,* in *The Expositor's Greek Testament,* II, p. 639. The basic work today is that of W. G. Kümmel, *Römer 7 und die Bekehrung des Paulus* (1929), who has been followed by the majority of German scholars. See references cited in Kümmel's *Man in the New Testament* (London: The Epworth Press, 1963), pp. 51-52. See also Barrett, *op. cit.,* pp. 140, 152; Goppelt, *op. cit.,* p. 146. Longenecker (*op. cit.,* pp. 114-116) includes with this interpretation "the human cry . . . of the spiritually sensitive."

58. Rudolf Bultmann, "Romans 7 and the Anthropology of Paul" in his *Existence and Faith,* ed. by Schubert M. Ogden (New York: Meridian Books, Inc., 1960), pp. 147-157.

59. Cf. Arndt and Gingrich, *Lexicon,* 266.

60. C. H. Dodd, "Ennomos Christou" in *Studia Paulina* (De Zwaan Festschrift, 1953), pp. 96-110, followed by Longenecker, *op. cit.,* pp. 183-

190, feels that the law of Christ is not the law of love but a body of traditional sayings of Jesus which provided an objective basis for Christian conduct. While the existence of such a tradition is established, we do not feel that the "law of Christ" is this tradition conceived as a new law for the Christian community.

V. WORD AND POWER (1 Corinthians 1:17—2:5)

William Childs Robinson, Jr.

1. Walter Bauer, *A Greek-English Lexicon of the New Testament and Other Early Christian Literature*, tr. by W. F. Arndt and F. W. Gingrich (1957), s.v.; Ulrich Wilckens, *Weisheit und Torheit* (Beiträge zur historischen Theologie, 26, 1959), 32 ff.

2. Johannes Weiss, *The History of Primitive Christianity*, 1937 (=*Earliest Christianity*, 1959), pp. 323 ff.; conveniently presented and ably criticized by John Coolidge Hurd, Jr., *The Origin of I Corinthians* (New York: Seabury Press, 1965), pp. 43-47.

3. Wilckens, *Weisheit und Torheit*, 5 ff.; 212 n. 5 criticism of Schmithals' de facto separation of 1 Cor. 1:17 ff. from the preceding verses.

4. *The New English Bible. New Testament* (Oxford University Press and Cambridge University Press, 1961).

5. Johannes Schneider, art. "σταυρός κτλ." in *Theologisches Wörterbuch zum Neuen Testament*, VII (1964), 575; cf. Ernst Käsemann, "Die Heilsbedeutung des Todes Jesu nach Paulus," *Zur Bedeutung des Todes Jesu* (Exegetische Beiträge, ed. Fritz Viering, 1967), 26.

6. Ernest De Witt Burton, *A Critical and Exegetical Commentary on the Epistle to the Galatians* (The International Critical Commentary, 1921), p. 145.

7. Justin, *Dialogue with Trypho*, 32; 89 f.

8. Schmithals, *Die Gnosis in Korinth* (Forschungen zur Religion und Literatur des Alten und Neuen Testaments, 66, 1956, 2nd ed. 1965); Wilckens, *Weisheit und Torheit;* art. "σοφία κτλ." in ThWNT, VII, 465 ff.

9. Schmithals, *Die Gnosis in Korinth*, 2nd ed., 130; Wilckens, *Weisheit und Torheit*, 205 ff.

10. See the review of Wilckens, *Weisheit und Torheit*, by Carsten Colpe, *Monatschrift für Pastoraltheologie*, 52 (1963), 487 ff., esp. 488 f.; and the criticism by Schmithals, *Die Gnosis in Korinth*, 2nd ed., 131.

11. In the reviews by Colpe (n. 10), Helmut Koester, *Gnomon*, 33 (1961), 590 ff. See also Hans Conzelmann, "Die Mutter der Weisheit," *Zeit und Geschichte: Dankesgabe an Rudolf Bultmann* (1964), 225 ff., esp. 226 f.; Conzelmann, "Paulus und die Weisheit," *New Testament Studies*, 12 (1965-66), 231 ff., esp. 235 ff.; A. D. Nock, "Gnosticism," *Harvard Theological Review*, 57 (1964), 255 ff.

12. Rightly maintained by Herbert Braun, *Qumran und das Neue Testament*, I (1966), 189.

13. Günther Bornkamm, *Studien zu Antike und Urchristentum: Gesammelte Aufsätze,* II, 2nd ed. (1963), 119 ff.

14. See my article, "The Church in the World," *Interpretation,* XIX (October, 1965), pp. 412-417.

15. Hurd, *op. cit.,* pp. 245, 281.

16. J. P. M. Sweet, "A Sign for Unbelievers: Paul's Attitude to Glossolalia," *NTS,* 13 (1966-67), 240 ff., esp. 253.

17. Schmithals, *Paulus und die Gnostiker* (Theologische Forschung, 35, 1965), 99 f.

18. E.g., 1 Cor. 15:1, 14; 1 Thess. 4:1; Gal. 1:8-9.

19. Hans Dieter Betz, *Nachfolge und Nachahmung Jesu Christi im Neuen Testament* (Beiträge zur historischen Theologie, 37, 1967), 154.

20. F. C. Baur and his school, see references in Schmithals, *Paulus und die Gnostiker,* 89 f.

21. Hurd, *op. cit.,* pp. 3 ff.

22. Hurd, *op. cit.,* pp. 295-296; Schmithals, *op. cit.,* 89 ff.

23. William Wrede, *Die Echtheit des zweiten Thessalonicherbriefs* (Texte und Untersuchungen zur Geschichte der altchristlichen Literatur, neue Folge, IX. Band, 2. Heft, 1903).

24. See the criticism by Werner Georg Kümmel, *Introduction to the New Testament,* tr. by A. J. Mattill, Jr. (Nashville: Abingdon Press, 1966), p. 189.

25. *NTS,* 12 (1965-66), 231 ff., on 1 Cor. 1:18 ff., 236 ff.

26. 2 Cor. 5:21; 8:9; Gal. 4:4; Rom. 8:3; Phil. 2:6-8; on whether some of the "handed over" statements belong here see Werner Kramer, *Christ, Lord, Son of God,* Studies in Biblical Theology, 50; tr. by Brian Hardy (London: SCM Press Ltd., 1966), pp. 115 ff., and Wiard Popkes, *Christus Traditus* (Abhandlungen zur Theologie des Alten und Neuen Testaments, 49, 1967), 201 ff.

27. Rudolf Bultmann, *Theology of the New Testament,* tr. by Kendrick Grobel (New York: Charles Scribner's Sons, 1951), I, 293-294.

28. Cf. Koester's comment, *Gnomon* 33 (1961), 592, that for Paul the cross was a metaphor for the historicity of all revelation.

29. Betz, *Nachfolge und Nachahmung,* 168, referring to Käsemann, *Exegetische Versuche und Besinnungen,* I (2nd ed., 1960), 91.

30. Betz, 176 f.

31. *Ibid.,* 182 f.

32. *Ibid.,* 187 f.

VI. LAMPADES IN MATTHEW 25:1-13

Joachim Jeremias

1. Mekh. Ex., 19:17. (See Jeremias, *Parables of Jesus,* Scribner, 1955.) Midhr. Esther 1:4.

Unfortunately we are given no further help by Pesiq. r. 43, ed. Freidmann, Vienna, 180 b, 8. Billerbeck translates the passage as follows: "R. Jᵉhuda b. Zᵉbida (around 250) said: 'When he took her to himself again after she was set free, Amram placed Jochebed in a sedan chair (פיריא [sic! read פוריא]). Ahron went on one side and Mirjam went on the other. They carried torches and danced before her' " (I 510). Like others before him, Billerbeck apparently derives the *hapax legomenon* קורקנות (which, by the way, is missing from the parallel texts b. Sota 12a; b.B.B. 120a and Ex. r. 1–2.1), translated by him with "torches," from κηρίων (wax-candle). But quite apart from the fact that the translation would then have to be "candles" instead of "torches," this derivation is invalidated by the arrangement of the consonants. The same objection can be made to M. Jastrow's suggested translation "castanets," derived from the word קירקור "to shake" (*A Dictionary of the Targumim, the Talmud Babli and Yerushalmi, and the Midrashic Literature*, New York, 1886–1903, 1370a). The only etymologically satisfactory translation is "herald's staff" (κηρύκιον). This translation is suggested by M. Güdemann, *Lexidion der Fremdwörter* (Anhang zur Ausgabe Wien 1880 von Pesiq. r., 205b) and by G. Dalman, *Aramäisch-neuhebräisches Handwörterbuch*, Frankfurt a.M. ²1922, 392 b.

2. This applied also to lampstands. See below.

3. Aeschylus, *Agamemnon* 8.

4. Daniel 5:5 θ.

5. Judith 10:22.

6. P. Oxy. XII 1449, 19 (213-217 A.D.).

7. Mark 4:21 (par. Matt. 5:15; Luke 8:16; 11:33); Matt. 6:22 (par. Luke 11:34); Luke 11:36; 12:35; 15:8; John 5:35.

8. j. Schabb. 2.4d, 5-10: through the night until early morning.

9. This was still my own interpretation in the 6th edition of *Die Gleichnisse Jesu* (Göttingen, 1962), 174 (cf. *The Parables of Jesus*, 1954, p. 132). "Cresset" is the interpretation of K. Galling, *Die Beleuchtungsgeräte im israelitisch-jüdischen Kulturgebiet*, ZDPV 46 (1923), 32.

10. Kel. 2.4; b. Ber. 53b and ö.

11. Mekh. Ex. on 13.21 (Mekh. Schim'on b. Jochai ed. Epstein-Melamed, Jerusalem 1955, 47.21; Mekh. Jischma"el. ed. Horovitz-Rabin, Jerusalem ²1960, 82.6).

12. H. Heyne, *Das Gleichnis von den klugen und törichten Jungfrauen. Eine literarisch-ikonographische Studie zur altchristlichen Zeit* (Leipzig 1922), illustrations pp. 8-10. F. Zorell, *De lampadibus decem virginum, Verbum Domini* (1930), 179-181.

13. *Kennst Du das Land? Bilder aus dem gelobten Lande zur Erklärung der heiligen Schrift* (Leipzig ¹⁸1899), 188. Cf. L. Schneller, *Evangelienfahrten. Bilder aus dem Leben Jesu in der Beleuchtung des Heiligen Landes* (Leipzig ⁷1899), 456. Zorell, *op. cit.*, 181 f., and following him, P. Gaechter, *Das Matthäusevangelium*, Innsbruck-Wien-München (1964), 799-803, deserve the credit for rescuing Schneller's observations from oblivion.

14. We have to do, in other words, with so-called "natural" torches as dis-

tinguished from "receptacle" torches, which consisted of metal pans mounted on shafts. Both kinds of torches are called אֲבוּקָה. If one wanted to distinguish the receptacle torches from the natural torches, he called them לַפִּיד?. (Cf. S. Krauss, *Talmudische Archäologie* I, Leipzig, 1910, 68.)

15. *Arbeit und Sitte in Palästina* IV (Gütersloh, 1935), 269. It is difficult to understand why Dalman nevertheless two pages later interprets the λαμπάδες in Matt. 25:1 ff. as lamps (271).

16. Schneller, *Evangelienfahrten,* 456.

17. Schneller, *Kennst Du das Land?,* 188; *Evangelienfahrten,* 455.

18. Gaechter, *op. cit.,* 802.

19. Th. Zahn, *Das Evangelium des Matthäus* (Leipzig-Erlangen ⁴1922), 679, n. 32.

20. L. Bauer, *Volksleben im Lande der Bibel* (Leipzig, 1903), 90; H. Granquist, *Marriage Conditions in a Palestinian Village* II (Helsingfors, 1935), 65; Gaechter, *op. cit.,* 800.

21. b. Ber. 51ab; b. Quid. 70ab. Billerbeck is correct in picturing the bride as sitting modestly at the side of the bridegroom at the wedding table (I 505). The documentation he produces in I 515 (Pes. 7.13: "A bride must turn her face away when she eats") refers not to a wedding celebration but to the Passover feast—specifically to the frequent case when in a crowded city two families celebrate in the same room. Then a newly married woman must be careful that her face is not seen by the members of the other group.

22. On the torch dance at the Feast of the Tabernacles compare Sukka 5.4; Tos. Sukka 4.2 (198.9); j. Sukka 5.55c, 2; b. Sukka 51b; 53a.

VII. WORLD IN MODERN THEOLOGY
AND IN NEW TESTAMENT THEOLOGY
James M. Robinson

1. *ZZ,* III (1925), 337 f., reprinted in *Anfänge der dialektischen Theologie,* I, 51.

2. Martin Heidegger, *Sein und Zeit,* 148.

3. *Ibid.*

4. Rudolf Bultmann, *Theology of the New Testament* (New York: Charles Scribner's Sons, 1955), II, p. 237.

5. Heidegger, *op. cit.,* 146.

6. *Ibid.*

7. Bultmann, *op. cit.,* I, p. 191.

8. Friedrich Schleiermacher, "Zweites Sendschreiben an Lücke," *Theologische Studien und Kritiken,* II (1829), 481 ff., reprinted in his *Sämmtliche Werke,* I. Abt., 2. Bd. (1836), 605-653.

9. *SW,* I, 2, 605 ff.

10. *Ibid.,* I, 2, 607.

11. Bultmann, *op. cit.,* I, Part Two, pp. 185 ff.

12. *SW,* I, 2, 627 ff.

13. *Ibid.,* I, 2, 627.

14. *Ibid.*, 629 f.

15. *Ibid.*, 611.

16. *Ibid.*, 631.

17. Schleiermacher, *Der christliche Glaube* (6. unveränderte Ausgabe, 1884), I, 14, par. 4.

18. *ThStKr*, II (1829), 225 ff.; *SW*, I, 2, 577-604, esp. 584.

19. *SW*, I, 2, 586.

20. Rudolf Otto, *Kant-Friessche Religionsphilosophie* (1909).

21. Wilhelm Bousset, *ThR*, XII (1909), 471-488.

22. Cf. *RGG*, 2nd ed., IV, 499 f.

23. Karl Barth, *Revolutionary Theology in the Making*, tr. by James D. Smart (Richmond: John Knox Press, 1964), pp. 89-90.

24. Bousset, *Kyrios Christos*, 1921, XV; 5th ed., 17 f.

25. *ChrW*, XXXVI (1922), 320; reprinted in *Anfänge der dialektischen Theologie*, I, 119.

26. *SW*, I, 2, 585.

27. *Der christliche Glaube*, I, 153, par. 30.

28. *SW*, I, 2, 611.

29. *Der christliche Glaube*, I, 152, par. 30.

30. Schleiermacher, *Nebenformen, SW*, I, 2, 627.

31. *SW*, I, 2, 631.

32. Heidegger, *Holzwege*, 55.

33. *Op. cit.*, 311.

34. Karl Barth, *Kirchliche Dogmatik*, III, 2 (1948), 534.

35. "Das Problem der Hermeneutik," *ZThK*, XLVII (1950), 68; *GuV*, II, 234 f.; *Essays Philosophical and Theological*, pp. 259 f.

36. *ZThK*, LXXXVII (1962), 8; *GuV*, IV (1965), 192.

37. *Interpretation*, XVIII (1964), pp. 358 f.; *Kerygma und historischer Jesus*, 2. Aufl., 141 f., n. 43; 195, n. 6.

38. *ZThK*, LX (1963), 341; *GuV*, IV, 119 f.

39. In my *Kerygma und historischer Jesus* (1960), 160, 2nd ed. (1965), 198.

40. Ernst Fuchs, "Das Zeitverständnis Jesu," *Zur Frage nach dem historischen Jesus, Ges. Aufs.* II (1960), 304-376, and previously in his *Hermeneutik* (1954), 224.

41. Gerhard Ebeling, *Theologie und Verkündigung, Hermeneutische Untersuchungen zur Theologie* I (1962), 47: "self-understanding—and that is meant in the sense of a comprehensive understanding of reality."

42. Hans-Georg Gadamer, "Hermeneutik und Historismus," *PhR*, IX (1966), 258; *Wahrheit und Methode*, 2. Aufl. (1965), 493 f.

43. *WuM*, 474-476.

44. Schleiermacher, *Existentialverhältnis, SW*, I, 2, 586.

45. Schleiermacher, *Glaubenslehre*, 1. Teil, 1. Abschnitt.

46. Hans Jonas, *Der Begriff der Gnosis* (1930), 11, reprinted in *Gnosis und spätantiker Geist*, II, 1 (1954), 9 f.

47. Bultmann, *Kerygma and Myth*, I, pp. 17-22.

48. James M. Robinson, *Kerygma und historischer Jesus* (1967), 141-145.

49. Van A. Harvey and Schubert M. Ogden, "How New Is the 'New Quest of the Historical Jesus'?" in *The Historical Jesus and the Kerygmatic Christ*, tr. and ed. by Carl E. Braaten and Roy A. Harrisville (Nashville: Abingdon Press, 1964), pp. 197-242.

50. Bultmann, *GuV*, I, 84.

51. Jonas, *Augustin und das paulinische Freiheitsproblem*, 1930, 2. Aufl. (1965), 84.

52. As Bultmann explains in the *Haenchen-Festschrift Apophoreta*, *Beiheft* 30 to *ZNW* (1964), 69, and not without reason—cf. the anthropological point of departure in Paul's own attempt to systematize his theology, his Letter to the Romans.

53. William Wrede, *Paulus* (1905).

54. Wrede, *Das Messiasgeheimnis in den Evangelien* (1901).

55. Martin Werner, *Der Einfluss paulinischer Theologie im Markusevangelium*, *Beiheft* 1 to *ZNW* (1923).

56. Cf. the series of essays by Martin Dibelius, collected posthumously in his *Aufsätze zur Apostelgeschichte* (1951), followed up by Philipp Vielhauer, "Zum 'Paulinismus' der Apostelgeschichte," *EvTh*, X (1950), 1-15; and Ernst Haenchen's Meyer commentary on Acts (1956).

57. For this shift in Johannine studies dating from Percival Gardner-Smith, *St. John and the Synoptic Gospels* (1938), see Ernst Haenchen, "Johanneische Probleme," *ZThK*, LVI (1959), 19-54; *Gott und Mensch* (1965), 78-113.

58. Bultmann, *Theology of the New Testament*, II, pp. 3-14.

59. Günther Gawlick in *PhR*, X (1962), 299-302.

60. *BhTh*, 26 (1959).

61. Cf. Carsten Colpe, *Jahrbuch für Antike und Christentum*, VII (1964), 79.

62. *RGG*, 3rd ed., II (1958), col. 1652.

63. *JAC*, VII (1964), 93.

64. Martin Krause, "Der Stand der Veröffentlichung der Nag Hammadi Texte," *The Origins of Gnosticism*, ed. by Ugo Bianchi (Supplement XII to *Numen*, 1967), pp. 61-88, esp. pp. 74-77.

65. Hans Jonas, in *The Bible in Modern Scholarship*, ed. by J. Philip Hyatt (Nashville: Abingdon Press, 1965), pp. 279-293.

VIII. JOHN CALVIN'S POLEMIC AGAINST IDOLATRY

John H. Leith

1. This theme is central not only in the work of John Calvin but also in the theology of Professor William Childs Robinson, and hence is appropriate in a volume honoring him.

Paul Tillich observed that ". . . a central attitude and doctrine of Calvinism [is] . . . the fear of idolatry. This is tremendously strong in him.

Calvin fights the idols wherever he believes he sees them. He is not interested in the history of religion, which is practically condemned as a whole as being idolatrous. Religion cannot help having an idolatrous element. Religion is a factory of idols all the time. Therefore the Christian and the theologian must be on his guard and prevent idolatrous trends from overwhelming his relationship to God.

"He fights against the pictures in the churches, *all* kinds of things which can divert the mind from the merely transcendent God. This is the reason for the sacred emptiness of the Calvinist church buildings. There is always a fear of idolatry in the depths of men who have overcome idolatry. So it was with the prophets, so it was with the Arabians (Islam), so it was now with the Reformers. Calvinism is an iconoclastic movement—crushing icons, idols, pictures of all kinds, because they deviate from God Himself." (Paul Tillich, *A History of Christian Thought* [ed. by Peter H. John, 2nd edition, 1956], p. 216.)

2. Heinrich Heppe, *Ursprung und Geschichte der Bezeichnungen 'reformierte' und 'lutherische' Kirche* (Gotha, 1859), 28.

3. Alexander Schweizer, *Die Glaubenslehre der Evangelisch—Reformierten Kirche dargestellt und aus den Quellen belegt* (Zurich: Orell, Füssli und Comp, 1844), I, 45.

4. John Calvin, *Institutes of the Christian Religion,* ed. by John T. McNeill, tr. by Ford Lewis Battles, Vols. XX and XXI of the *Library of Christian Classics* (Philadelphia: The Westminster Press, 1960), I, i, 1, 2. Reference to this work hereafter cited by book, chapter, and paragraph reference; e.g., I, i, 1.

5. "Religion is not some artifice of priests; and idolatry, the worship of contingent elements in history as the ultimate centers of meaning, is not some aberration of religion which could be eliminated if religion were destroyed. What is known as religion is simply Man's effort to come to terms with his situation of finiteness and freedom. Since Man transcends both nature and himself he is bound to seek for a principle of meaning which will give coherence to his world, beyond nature and himself. Since Man is finite and involved in nature he is bound to express his sense of the ultimate in less than ultimate terms. That is, he makes god in his own image and his god therefore comes in conflict with other gods made in the image of other men and other civilizations and cultures; and the conflict is brutal beyond the brutality of animal life because unconditioned claims are made for these conditioned values. This is a permanent and perennial problem of human history and it reveals itself with equal clarity whether the religious element is explicit or only implicit and whether men are consciously religious or have consciously disavowed traditional religion." (Reinhold Niebuhr, "Religion and Action" in *Science and Man,* ed. by Ruth Nanda Anshen [New York: Harcourt, Brace and Company, Inc., 1942], p. 48.)

6. Kilian McDonnell, OSB, *John Calvin, The Church and the Eucharist* (Princeton, N. J.: Princeton University Press, 1967), p. 161.

7. I, xi, 1.

8. I, xi, 8. "All we conceive concerning God in our own minds is an insipid fiction." (I, xi, 4.)

9. *Corpus Reformatorum: Joannis Calvini Opera Quae Supersunt Omnia,* ed. by Guilielmus Baum, Eduardus Cunitz, and Eduardus Reuss (Brunsvigae: C. A. Schwetschke et Filium, 1863-1897), XXVII: 253 (a reference to this work is cited hereafter by *CR,* followed by volume number and column number; e.g., *CR* XXVII:253): "Et auiourd'huy quand les Papistes diront qu'il faut punir les heretiques: cela est vray, nous confessons qu'ils le meritent. Mais cependant il falloit venir à cest article qui est ici contenu: c'est assavoir que nous ayons cogneu quel est le Dieu auquel nous servons, que nous soyons bien asseurez que ce n'est point à l'aventure que nostre religion a esté publiee: mais que nous tenons la verité infaillible que Dieu nous a envoyee, et qu'on nous l'annonce en son nom, et en son authorité: que c'est en luy que nostre foy est fondee. Il nous falloit (di-ie) là venir. Or les Papistes s'abrutissent là dessus, qu'il leur semble qu'en se fermant les yeux ils pourront executer leur rage, et furie contre les innoncens." In assessing the significance of this statement, it must be remembered that much of Calvin's theology proclaims the impotence of force in religious matters.

10. I, xi, 9.

11. I, xii, 1.

12. I, xii, 3. Schubert Ogden has recently written the following: ". . . we must guard against a common misunderstanding. It is easy to suppose that idolatry means the diversion of faith wholly away from God himself to some merely nondivine thing falsely identified as divine. Actually, however, it is less that the idolater simply identifies the nondivine thing as God than that he regards it as having a unique significance as a symbol or sacrament of God's presence. His idol is for him the indispensable evidence of God's power and favor, and so, while his trust is indeed in God, it is not whole, but is finally divided between God himself and the idol. For this reason, the real issue of faith at the deepest, existential level is never *whether* we are to believe in God, or even, as is sometimes said, *what* God we are to believe in; the issue, instead, is *how* we are to believe in the only God in whom anyone can believe and in whom each of us somehow must believe. And here there are but the two possibilities clarified once for all by the Protestant Reformers: either we are so to believe in God that we finally place our trust in him *alone;* or else we are so to believe in him that we divide our ultimate trust by placing it in part in some idol alongside him." (Schubert M. Ogden, *The Reality of God* [New York: Harper & Row, 1966], pp. 23-24.)

13. I, xii, 1.

14. I, xi, 8.

15. I, iii, 1.

16. I, iii, 2.

17. *Ibid.*

18. I, iii, 1.

19. I, xi, 1.

20. I, xi, 6.

21. I, xi, 1.

22. I, xi, 7.

23. *CR* X, 403.

24. *CR* XLIX, 319 ff.

25. Léon Wencelius, *L'Esthétique de Calvin.* Paris: Société d'Edition "Les Belles Lettres," 1937, pp. 344 ff.

26. I, xi, 12.

27. I, xi, 7.

28. I, xi, 12.

29. McDonnell, *op. cit.,* p. 168.

30. IV, vii, 25.

31. Reinhold Niebuhr, *The Nature and Destiny of Man* (New York: Charles Scribner's Sons, 1943), II, p. 317.

32. IV, i, 21.

33. IV, i, 7.

34. Commentary on Acts 15:2 *CR* XLVIII, 340-341.

35. IV, xvii, 36.

36. *Calvin: Theological Treatises,* tr. by the Rev. J. K. S. Reid, Vol. XXII of the *Library of Christian Classics* (Philadelphia: The Westminster Press, 1954), p. 159.

37. II, xiii, 4.

38. E. David Willis, *Calvin's Catholic Christology,* Vol. II of *Studies in Medieval and Reformation Thought* (Leiden: E. J. Brill, 1966), p. 7.

39. IV, xviii, 7.

40. IV, xviii, 2.

41. II, viii, 17.

42. III, xx, 22.

43. III, xx, 29.

44. IV, x, 15, 24.

45. III, xx, 50.

46. III, xx, 15.

47. III, xx, 16.

48. III, xx, 5, 16.

49. III, xx, 4, 5, 6, 29.

50. IV, x, 29. Cf. Francis M. Higman, *The Style of John Calvin in His French Polemical Treatises* (New York: Oxford University Press, 1967), pp. 155 ff.

51. IV, x, 12.

52. McDonnell, *op. cit.,* p. 133.

53. III, xx, 33.

54. III, xx, 32.

55. Peter Barth and Wilhelm Niesel, *Joannis Calvini Opera Selecta* (Monachii in Aedibus: Chr. Kaiser, 1952), II, 31 ff.

56. *Ibid.*, p. 17.

57. III, xx, 5, 15-16.

58. W. H. Auden, "For the Time Being, A Christmas Oratorio," in *The Collected Poetry of W. H. Auden* (New York: Random House, 1945), p. 444.

IX. THEOLOGICAL PERSUASION

T. F. Torrance

1. Michael Polanyi, *Personal Knowledge* (Chicago: The University of Chicago Press, 1958), p. 151.

2. *Ibid.*, pp. 280 ff.

3. C. F. von Weizäcker, *The World View of Physics,* tr. by Marjorie Grene (London: Routledge and Kegan Paul, 1952), p. 132.

4. 2 Corinthians 5:20, KJV.

TABULA GRATULATORIA

The following friends of Dr. William Childs
Robinson join in expressing gratitude for his
life of devoted service to Christ:

Gabriel Abdullah
John Nance Akers
John William Aldridge
George A. Anderson
O. M. Anderson
James T. Anderton
Samuel G. Andreasen
Mrs. Elizabeth Phifer Armfield
Walter D. Arnold
John N. Ashenfelder
Stuart Barton Babbage
Steve A. Bacon
Donald B. Bailey
J. Lewis Baker
Robert G. Balnicky
J. Richard Bass
Dwight S. Bayley
B. Clayton Bell
Mr. and Mrs.
  Wm. Henry Benchoff
C. Charles Benz, Jr.
Edward S. Berry, Jr.
Alfred L. Bixler
Marion A. Boggs
Jack W. Bowling
David G. Boyce

Robert F. Boyd
Cecil D. Brearley, Jr.
A. C. Bridges
William C. Brownson, Jr.
Vernon S. Broyles, Jr.
Harry H. Bryan
John C. Bryan
Allen Cabaniss
James S. Cantrell
John A. Cannon, Jr.
Mr. and Mrs. Sam S. Cappel
Samuel A. Cartledge
Knox Chamblin
Major Hayes Clark
Robert J. Coker, Jr.
Roy W. Coker
Columbia Seminary Student
  Body 1967-68
Mr. and Mrs.
  Thomas Erwin Cook
Mr. and Mrs.
  Jesse W. Cooke, Jr.
W. Creed Cooper
Charles B. Cousar
R. Wilbur Cousar
Donald M. Covington

Eleanor Cox
Newton Cox
Samuel Noel Cramer
John M. Crow
R. McFerran Crowe
John B. Danhof
J. Millen Darnell
C. Edward Davis
Frank B. Davis
Frederick C. Debele, Jr.
John B. Degges
John A. DeKruyter
Marshall B. Dendy
Ludwig R. Dewitz
Thomas M. Dews
Bonneau H. Dickson
John B. Dickson
Wilds S. DuBose, Sr.
Joel P. Easterling
T. Harry Eckhoff
Morris J. Ehrlich, III
Thomas E. Elkin
Marling Elliott
Thomas Talbot Ellis, Jr.
Henry A. Erion
Donald R. Esty
Allen E. Fortune
Charles N. Foshee
W. G. Foster, Jr.
Albert H. Freundt, Jr.
William E. Frisbee
C. Darby Fulton
James H. Gailey, Jr.
Robert M. Gant, Jr.
Paul L. Garber
Burns Gibbs
Alton H. Glasure

H. Walton Grady
Mrs. J. B. Green
Alva M. Gregg
Robert L. Griffin
Shirley C. Guthrie, Jr.
Ben Haden
Oliver N. Hamby
Mr. and Mrs. E. H. Hamilton
John Allen Hare
M. Douglas Harper, Jr.
Albert G. Harris, Jr.
Samuel T. Harris, Jr.
Woodfin G. Harry
Joseph S. Harvard, III
Stephen Thomas Harvin
William J. Hazelwood
Basil V. Hicks
James C. Hicks, Jr.
William F. Holderman, Jr.
T. W. Horton, Jr.
James M. Hovland
Gary Howell
Samuel B. Hoyt, Jr.
William R. Hoyt
James H. Huffaker
Edsel M. Huffstetler
Philip Edgcumbe Hughes
C. William Hull
Stephen M. Huntley, Jr.
George B. Hutchins
Shin Ishimaru
Erskine L. Jackson
Robert L. Jackson
Allen C. Jacobs
Mrs. John L. Jacobs
Agnes Irene Johnson
Otto Kay

Thomas G. Kay, Jr.
William Chester Keller
D. James Kennedy
D. Burke Kerr
George H. Kirker
Louis C. LaMotte
John S. Land
Richard G. Laurens
Frederick H. Leach
J. Miller Liston
David A. Long, III
George W. Long, Jr.
Eduard N. Loring
Richard L. Love
James S. Lowry
Gordon L. Lyle
Olof Halvard Lyon
Robert Milton Lytton
R. D. McCall
D. Sidney McCarty
David McCarty
Hugh W. McClure III
John T. McCrea
Thomas H. McDill
W. Ronald McElrath
William E. McElveen
Rob Roy McGregor, Jr.
Claude McIntosh
Dean G. McKee
M. A. Macdonald
J. A. Ross Mackenzie
Robert E. Malsbary
A. A. Markley, III
William H. Marquis
Arthur M. Martin
Mr. and Mrs. Joe Martin
Curtis W. Medlin

John W. Melton
P. D. Miller
Harold W. Minor, Jr.
Robert L. Montgomery
J. Fred Moore
Park Moore
Thomas G. Morris, Sr.
Frank Morse
Margaret Morse
Mr. and Mrs. W. L. Mosal, Jr.
Henry J. Mueller
Luther M. Mundy
Mr. and Mrs. W. D. Munson
Thomas J. Nash III
J. Boyce Nelson
R. L. Nelson
W. O. Nelson
Robert G. Newman
John T. Newton, Jr.
E. P. Nichols
H. Gudger Nichols, Jr.
W. D. O'Neal
J. Will Ormond
Richard W. Paddon
David L. Parks
John G. Parks
Stanford Parnell
Thomas R. Patete
J. G. Peck
B. E. Pettit
Wythe M. Peyton, Jr.
J. Davison Philips
Everett H. Phillips
Robert P. Piephoff
G. Thomas Preer
J. Fairman Preston, Sr.
John Pridgen

Harold B. Prince
R. Quinn Pugh
Robert Eugene Randolph
Sanders G. Read, Jr.
Paul David Reynolds, Sr.
William C. Rhodes, Jr.
J. McDowell Richards
James T. Richardson
John R. Richardson
Mr. and Mrs.
   David W. Robinson
Mr. and Mrs.
   George F. Robinson
Mr. and Mrs. H. B. Robinson
Henry S. Robinson
Mr. and Mrs. Jerry Robinson
Jonathan N. Robinson
Mr. and Mrs.
   R. Hoke Robinson
William C. Robinson, Jr.
John C. Ropp
Beryl G. Rosenberger
Jeb Russell
Frank M. Ryburn
John H. Sadler
Richard E. Sanner
Harry T. Schutte
Mr. and Mrs.
   Henry G. Schwartz
Mr. and Mrs.
   J. Julius Scott, Jr.
Leroy V. Secrest
Ernest T. Severs
Sterling Sexton
John D. Sharp
Angus R. Shaw III
Charles A. Sheldon III

T. Ellison Simpson
William C. Sistar, Sr.
J. B. Sloan
John Sloop
Sandy Sloop
Stephen J. Sloop, Jr.
Stephen J. Sloop, Sr.
James R. Smith
Morton H. Smith
James B. Stanford
Ray M. Stover
R. L. Summers
Richard K. Swayze
Lowell Beach Sykes
John Bilbra Talmage
B. Harrison Taylor
Leonard Jackson Taylor
T. Reichardt Taylor
Robert H. Teed
James M. Terrell
Fred D. Thompson, Jr.
William R. Thurman
Harry S. Topham
Neil E. Truesdell
Leonard T. Van Horn
Mrs. Ruth Suggs Varner
James B. Wagner
Reuben J. Wallace
Ronald S. Wallace
Hubert G. Wardlaw
Hubert G. Wardlaw, Jr
G. Dana Waters, III
John E. Watts, Jr.
Thurlow Weed
Albert N. Wells
C. W. Thomas West
Harold White

Robert A. White, Jr.
Zan White
James R. Wilburn
Norman E. Wilhelm
D. Doug Wilkinson
Sam Williams
Glen E. Williamson
Mr. and Mrs.
    E. Lee Willingham, III

Ronnie Isaac Willis
Robert Bruce Wills
William T. Wing, Jr.
Miles C. Wood, Jr.
George R. Wright
Ferman L. Young
J. Russell Young